LEPER FOR CHRIST

Brother Joshua, now a leper with only a few years to live, installed as the "'Lord of the Manor" of Khor Melang and looking the part.

LEPER FOR CHRIST

by **Aloysius Roche**

"This is the greatest love a man can shew, that he should lay down his life for his friends". John 15, 13.

Foreword by Cardinal Valerio Valeri

VERONA FATHERS
London – Cincinnati

Nihil obstat:

ANDREAS J. MOORE, L.C.L.
Censor deputatus

Imprimatur:

E. MORROGH BERNARD
Vic. Gen.

Westmonasterii, die 12a Novembris, 1962

Printed in Great Britain by Robert Cooke, London, E.7

FOREWORD

by

HIS EMINENCE CARDINAL VALERIO VALERI

The biography of Brother Joshua Dei Cas, known as the Leper of Khor-Melang, is a book such as has seldom come my way or been read with greater interest ; read all in one breath, I may say. And this in spite of the fact that, when I was Apostolic Delegate at Cairo, and was visiting the Verona Fathers in the sunny island of Gesira, I was frequently in contact with him, exchanging many a friendly greeting.

But the trouble with holy people is that their heroism is never properly appreciated, as long as they are actually engaged on the task of rearing the edifice of their spiritual life. The splendour of the building is hidden by the constructional work that is going on. And this is all the more so, when the humility of the architect has to be reckoned with, a humility prompting him to conceal the details of the operation.

Much, therefore, as I admired Brother Joshua when he was in the flesh, that admiration must have been immeasurably intensified had I known what I know now : that he was to fall a victim to his own apostolic charity, that his boundless affection for the negroes of Central Africa was to involve the sacrifice of his health and his life.

Over and above, I remained ignorant of many features of that life of his, so permeated with generosity and self-sacrifice, for the simple reason that they were camouflaged, so to say, by the habitual merriment of his disposition, and his engaging sense of humour : qualities which helped him to accept the painful trials that lay in store for him, and served as an incentive to his fellow-lepers to do the same.

No, indeed ! It is not every day that one makes the acquaintance of a man who ends his days as a leper among lepers and, nevertheless, insists that he is living in paradise : of a man who, at a comparatively early age, offers up his life in exchange for the life of a missionary colleague who was younger and stronger than himself.

Surely, then, the least I can do is to wish that this book may have an extensive circulation, and receive a warm welcome from the reading public. Many a pleasant hour may be spent in viewing the contrast, so well drawn out by the illustrious author, between Brother Joshua's slow and cumbersome physical constitution, and the lightning-like swiftness of his witty retorts and repartees. More important still, with such a shining example of Christian charity before them, readers can hardly fail to be stimulated to a more fervent service of God, and moved to praise Him for His mercy in permitting such masterpieces of His sanctifying grace to flourish amongst us.

Valerio Cardinal Valeri.

Rome, 23rd June, 1951.

8

1
THE MAN FROM THE MOUNTAINS

1

THE MAN FROM THE MOUNTAINS

AT five o'clock on the morning of April 25th, 1906, Brother Polionato, the *ostiarius,* rang the bell to rouse the community. That done, he unlocked the main door of the monastery as usual ; only, this time, he glanced outside just to see what kind of mood the weather was in.

"Santo Cielo ! what's the meaning of this !"

The *This* in question was a man, he might be anything between twenty or thirty, lying at full length and smiling away, as though he had as much right to be where he was as the step he had been sleeping on. The next minute he was up like a jump-jack.

'Pon my word, the door-keeper thought, what next ! These tramps are the limit . . . But no ; the suit this man was wearing was as good as new, though it certainly sat awkwardly upon him, and didn't seem to match the roughness of his general appearance. Besides, there was an attaché case by his side . . . Probably one of the strolling story-tellers, the gentlemen who go the round of presbyteries and convents telling the tale : a good job going begging at Brescia or Bergamo, all for the want of a few lire to pay the fare.

"What brings you here at this unearthly hour ?"

"I've come to be a missionary."

"But who let you into the grounds?"

"Nessuno. I climbed over the wall—last night. I've been here since, waiting for someone to open the door."

"Why didn't you ring the bell?"

"It was too late, you see. You were all in bed and I didn't want to disturb you."

This might be cheek or it might be simplicity; one hardly knew what to think.

"Where have you come from?"

The wall-climber waved his hand in the air. "From up yonder, from the Valtellina, from Piatta, one of the villages. I was born there."

Brother Polionato pricked up his ears; for, in that part of Italy, everyone who knows anything knows about the Valtellina, as notorious, in its own way, as Thermopylae or Glencoe, and for much the same reasons. It was at least 70 miles away as the crow flies.

"How did you manage to get to Verona?" was the next question.

For answer, the stranger began stamping up and down. "These are what carried me," he said, "at least some of the way, my two big feet."

And they were big feet, in all conscience, when one came to examine them, the biggest single parts of the man, really, with the possible exception of his head, which was on the large side as well.

"But you are not expected, are you?"

"Yes, I think so. I wrote to the Father Superior some while since, and he wrote back to our parish priest telling him to send me along."

"Cosa? Why didn't you say so at first? Come along.

Just wait in the parlour and I shall tell the Superior. And, by the way, what's your name?"

"Dei Cas, that's my name: Joshua Dei Cas."

"Very well. Sit down, will you, until he is able to see you."

Joshua did as he was told and let his eyes wander round the room. Some of us can remember these convent parlours of sixty or seventy years ago: a crucifix on the wall, a portrait of the Founder on the mantlepiece and a couple of plain chairs: otherwise almost bare, no doubt as a tactful reminder to the visitors that naked they came into the world, and naked they must leave it again, and sooner, perhaps, than they were inclined to suspect.

It was true enough; he had been invited. This religious Institute needed lay-brothers almost as much as it needed priests. The right sort, some of them with skilled trades and all of them able-bodied and willing, are a plain necessity to foreign missionary Orders generally, more especially to this one which was still in its infancy, you might say, having been canonically erected only forty years before.

When at last the head of the house made his appearance, he greeted Joshua cordially and took him along to the chapel where, no doubt, the young man's venture into the unknown was committed, once again, to the care of Him Who was its inspiration, and had been at the bottom of all such ventures for a matter of nineteen hundred years. Could he have foreseen what was in store for him, he might not have changed his

➜

IN THE VALTELLINA. Piatta, Brother Joshua's native village, on the right; Bormio, seven hundred feet below, on the left. In the background, the Stelvio mountain overshadowing the Pass.

mind, but he must have prayed harder than ever.

In the refectory, some minutes later, while Joshua was tackling a hearty breakfast, the Superior looked him over and asked a few leading questions.

There was no mistaking the class to which he belonged or his place of origin : these hefty hands gnarled and roughened by heavy manual labour, these broad shoulders surmounting a small body, that face chafed by Alpine winds and tanned by the strong suns of the summer. His movements were slow and ungainly, as though he had been used to working at dangerous heights, where a false step might end in injury or death. And so it turned out ; for it appeared that, for six months in the year, he had been a farm-hand, and for the other six, one of a gang of navvies whose job it was to keep the Stelvio Pass open against the snow-drifts and avalanches. ✗ here

He was a silent individual by custom ; that was easily seen. There was nothing to be got from him except by way of cross-examination. And, like most shy people, his answers, when they came, were clipped and jaunty, with a flavour of flippancy about them, a flippancy which, very likely, was only the nervousness of those who are seldom in contact with persons above their own station. Or, it might be that, what sounded like arrogance, was no more than the manliness of these sturdy hill-dwellers, to whose nature and trad-itions kow-towing and obsequiousness are foreign commodities. And, of course, the Valtellinese ; well, they did have some right to be jaunty, these people

←

The birthplace of a hero and a possible saint. Going towards the BURAT where the Dei Cas farm is situated, approx. five thousand feet high, where the sturdy family grew up.

13

who wore "upon their foreheads clear, the freedom of the mountaineer."

But then, the assault on the enclosure wall, and in the small hours, too : what was one to make of that ? True, this forced entry business wasn't exactly a novelty, an unheard of thing. There were cases, to be sure, some of them involving those who were now canonized saints. St. Clare of Assisi, for instance, who defied all the conventions by arriving at midnight and by the light of torches ; and St. Gerard Majella, an incorrigible squatter and gate-crasher, who spent months harrying superiors and lying down at doors, until those in charge threw up the sponge.

And wasn't there some highly placed Somebody or Other who was supposed to have said that if worldly folk knew the happiness to be found in cloisters, they would do exactly what this Joshua dei Cas had done the night before ?

There was a plain honesty about the man for all his uncouthness. And he had the untired eager look of those who are accustomed to a routine of exertion, and are ready to take on almost anything without being asked twice. There was no doubt, either, about his morals or his piety : his parish-priest had been emphatic on that point. At any rate, time would show.

And time was going to show with a vengeance. A day was coming, in fact, when missionaries of tried virtue and experience were to look with envious eyes upon this man from the mountains, when those in authority were to hold him up as an example to the whole Order. He was to live for another twenty-seven years, mostly spent among the Negroes of Central Africa, and he was to die the death of a leper. But even with all

14

the ravages of that disease upon him, he was to remain true to himself, and true to the Master whose hands had helped to hoist him over the nine foot wall of a monastic enclosure : two very great achievements.

The day following he wrote home to inform his parents and brothers of his safe arrival. This was the first of a long series of letters which were to reach these working people during the next three decades, and were to prove a veritable stand-by amid the ups and downs of their hard life. For this untrained son of the soil, contrary to all the known rules, could handle a pen with the same assurance with which he handled a pick and a shovel.

And so, there and then, Joshua Dei Cas was admitted among the members of the Institute of the Verona fathers, a mixed community of priests and lay-brothers, and of those preparing to become either the one or the other. His was the status of a postulant, literally one *asking* for admission, hoping to become, before many weeks, a proper novice, that is to say a beginner, or freshman, getting to know the ins and outs of the religious life.

In the earlier days of monasticism, he would have been left lying on the step for three days and nights, and even longer ; fasting and praying, meanwhile, and having his patience tested by the door-keeper who would, from time to time, open up, abuse the candidate for all he was worth, and tell him to clear out. Hence the name given to postulants, at that period, *pulsantes* or knockers. St. Benedict modified this custom, allowing the postulants to be taken inside, and kept for five days in a cell set aside for the purpose. After that, they were assigned to the quarters specially reserved for the novices. In his Order, the novitiate lasts for a year, and this is now the accepted term nearly everywhere.

In a modern monastery, postulants or novices mix in together and are subject to the same routine and the same Novice Master. Raw recruits, that is what they are; but, the former also *look* like raw recruits, since they wear their ordinary lay-clothes, and only assume the habit when their short postulancy is over. Meanwhile, neither are in any sense committed, since the vows are not taken until the novitiate, the probationary and training period, has been completed, when the novice becomes a professed religious.

2

IN THE VALTELLINA

THE train running between Lecco and Sondrio hugs the southern shore of the Lago di Como for several miles, before making a sharp turn to the right and proceeding to its destination. The gleaming stretch of water is no longer in sight ; but the passengers, if they are sitting on the left, may catch a glimpse of a wide valley, some sixty miles long, surrounded by hills and dotted with chestnut groves, vineyards and fields of maize. The river Adda, scrambling down from the Alps, winds and twists like a serpent along its whole length before entering the lake, from which it emerges again to join the Po in the vicinity of Cremona.

This is Valtellina, the Teglio Valley, Teglio being its one-time capital ; a rugged region, broken up by cliffs and primitive tracks, diversified with villages and small farms and, in the distance, forests extending right up into the heart of the mountains : the Highlands of Italy, you might say, with one of its Passes nearly twice the height of Ben Nevis.

Further down, Como, Lecco, Bergamo, Brescia and Verona trail out like a line of sentinels guarding its southern approaches. The little towns in the Valley itself are attractive enough and much-frequented by tourists : Bormio, famed for its hanging glaciers, and its cobbled streets running between houses with balconies and painted façades, Morbegno, equally famed for its mulberries and silk products, and Tirano, two miles from the Swiss frontier, boasting an ancient shrine, the Madonna di Tirano, and overshadowed by the memory of the massacre that took place during the religious wars of the early seventeenth century.

The natives are a proud and hardy race, and no wonder. What amount of Celtic blood, if any, remains in their veins, it is impossible to say. But this entire region was originally the domain of the Cisalpine Gauls who, for years on end, faced up to the legions of Rome and only lost their independence in 43 B.C. Como, Brescia, Verona and Milan were Gaulish cities in their time and for a long time.

Then, towards the close of the Middle Ages, strife and aggression were let loose upon the inhabitants who, at that date, amounted to no more than thirty thousand souls. The farmers were compelled to become fighters in their own defence. They proved to be such good fighters that the great European powers drew from the Valtellina some of their best recruits. Amid the rivalries and struggles that went on for something like a century, these thirty thousand hardly knew from one year to another whose chicks they were supposed to be. Milan was in charge for a while and, then, from 1513 onwards, the Swiss took over; that is to say, the confederation of villages known as the Grisons or Grey Leagues. This move led to quarrels and to the worst kind of quarrels, religious quarrels, with Protestant rulers on the one hand, and Catholic subjects on the other. The excesses are to be deplored; but they were not confined to one side. In 1619 there was open revolt followed by the massacre.

This painful episode has to be viewed in its general

context of aggression and counter-aggression ; and it is now conceded that the behaviour of the Swiss was provocative in the extreme. At any rate, whether true or false, the version of the incident still accepted in the Valley, is to the effect that in the face of what they conceived to be an attempt to take their religion from them by force, the natives seized the only weapons they could lay their hands on, and set about their opponents. Hence, to their descendants, the massacre is still known as the *Sacro Macello*.

Another tradition brings the Blessed Virgin into the field : Our Lady of Tirano who, so the story goes, appeared to one Amadeus, a farmer, and assured him that she was on the side of the peasants. There seems to be no official cult of Blessed Amadeus, although he is still venerated at the shrine of the pilgrimage church.

At this juncture, Spain stepped in. To them, the possession of the Valley was a strategic necessity. With France and Venice blocking the Passes on the west and east, this was the only route to the Rhine and the Netherlands open to the troops disembarking at Genoa and holding Milan. With the advent of that paradoxical and bitter conflict, the Thirty Years War, a Spanish garrison was established at Lecco. These were the soldiers described by Manzoni in *The Betrothed*, who "taught modesty to the wives and daughters of the town and, towards the end of summer, never failed to scatter themselves among the vineyards, to thin out the grapes and lighten, for the peasants, the labours of the vintage."

For years, neither side would give way. "The worst diseases," Richelieu noted in his Memorandum, "are those with complications, and the Valtellina Business is one of these. It involves Flanders, Germany and France itself."

With all this behind him by way of background, perhaps our Joshua might have been forgiven if there was some suggestion of swagger about his demeanour. One of his own confrères has testified that he always carried his head high and his mouth half open.

His father, Anacleto Dei Cas, had been a policeman in Bergamo for a number of years, but he resigned and decided to settle down for good as a farmer in the Valtellina. If you start from Bormio and go eastwards, crossing the pack-horse bridge spanning a torrent and then following a cart-track, you come to Piatta, which stands four thousand feet above sea-level. A mile or so beyond this village, there is a cluster of cottages known as the Burat. This was the place chosen and here Joshua was born in the year 1880 ; a smallholding situated in a rocky and generally barren area, with here and there fields and patches of arable land. It was a freehold bought with money paid down like nearly all the farms in the district ; a few acres, a few cows, a few pigs, a few poultry, that was the usual thing. But vines could be planted on the hillsides ; in fact, the wine of the Valley is of particularly good quality even for Italy.

If there were no olives, chestnuts were to be had for the picking. These roasted or boiled were the recognised breakfast food, especially for the children, who ate them on their way to school. For the other meals, it was pollenta and pollenta and pollenta again. There was practically no fish to be had, and no game except hares, wild goats and the chamois. Spaghetti was only for those down south and Risotto was a

Milanese dish. Cheese was an important product of the district as a whole. As for beef and mutton, they appeared on the table four or five times a year. At Christmas, the pigs were killed and the salami or sausages—and such sausages!—kept the family going half the year.

No doubt, then as now, tourists and a certain type of press-reporters came here, looked around for an hour or so, and then returned to the bosom of the opulent society from which they set out, charged to the brim with mutterings and wailings about "the appalling conditions in which these wretches are compelled to live." The trouble is that these slap-dash critics are usually handicapped by their own arbitrary and artificial presuppositions. Habituated to a certain "standard of living," an expression often used but seldom analysed, they naturally recoil at the sight of those who have to make-do and mend without the hundred and one accessories which we are used to over here. From this reaction, it is an easy transition to the conclusion that the people concerned must be recoiling in the same way and all the time.

Peace and quiet, composure and self-containment may be little to the taste of such critics, but quite a number of sane people still regard them as blessings. And there is more to it than that. Peasants generally feed well and sleep well. And they sleep often, by all accounts, knocking off for a nap when they feel like it, with no one to say them nay. They live rough, certainly, and live surrounded by dirt, the healthy dirt of the fields and the byres. But, at the time we are writing about, those who were looking for squalor and near-starvation had no need to go searching for it abroad. There was plenty of it to be found in their own fine cities. Destitution and squalor are, in the main, town products, not country ones.

If the Dei Cas family was anything of a sample, there was plenty of fun and laughter to be got out of three acres and a cow, and genuine fun and laughter at that : games and excursions without end during the long evenings, stories told to the crackling of the logs when the dark nights set in, and readings by the light of those little boat-shaped lamps which were in use until the arrival of electricity.

With the coming of spring, there was a general exodus to the pasture-lands lying farther up, where the family lived in make-shift accommodation to keep an eye on the cattle. Blue skies and hot suns, the frosty air laden with the scent of pine trees ; and, far off, the Alps with their "silent pinnacles of aged snow." And for sounds, bells and more bells ; the sharp clink of the sheep-bells on the hillsides, the deeper tones of the cow-bells at their very door and, three times a day from all the village belfries, the Gabriel bell with its age-long message of hope and consolation.

To say nothing of the mountains, those nurseries of the brave and the strong, which poets have been rhapsodising about for any number of years. "That noble architecture designed not only to astonish our minds, but also to delight and sanctify our hearts . . . The feeding of the rivers and the purifying of the winds are the least services they perform. To satisfy our thirst for the beauty of God's working is their highest mission . . . Here are silence, solitude and leisure—all that one needs as food for the soul." And so on.

In the numerous letters written home from Africa, Joshua never tired of casting a wistful glance in the direction of Piatta, never tired of impressing on his

23

brothers and sister that they did not realise how fortunate they were to be living high up among their mountains, with an air about them "potent enough to revive a corpse."

The very privations these small farmers were subjected to served them well in the struggle for existence ; unlike certain warriors of old, they went into the fight unhampered by showy and useless ornaments. Under God, Joshua owed everything to the training he had received in his family, on the farm and up on the Stelvio Pass working by his father's side ; and he made no bones about it. His strength of mind and of will, his disciplined body, his powers of endurance, the hardihood which enabled him to take everything in his stride, including the formidable disease that killed him —the foundations of all this were well and truly laid amid the rugged conditions of life in the Valtellina.

Anacleto and Matilda Conclini, his wife, were an upright couple, respected by the neighbours for their honesty and charity. "The family as a whole are a good example of the Christian way of living": that was the testimonial given by the parish priest, Don Michael Molinari. They were tolerant people and, in the home, pretty well everything was tolerated except insolence and deceit.

But Joshua was the flower of the flock, remarkable for the naïveté of his countenance and for his religious enthusiasm. He was already serving daily Mass, at an age when he could hardly shift the Missal from one side of the altar to the other. Up before five, winter and summer, he would be off at top speed, leaping over the burns and the boulders, and arriving out of breath at the door of the church.

When he was nine, he made his first communion.

Swift and impetuous by nature, he had gobbled up his lessons and homework while the other pupils were still biting at their pencils. At that time, education for the children of the peasants went no farther than the third class in an elementary school, and Joshua had To fall into line with the others. If his schooling was short, he had at least learnt to read and, for the next dozen years and more, reading was his sole recreation. His young sister Teresina, said later that she never remembered seeing him at the table without some book or magazine in his hand. It was this habit, in fact, that paved the way for his vocation, for his departure from the Valley, and for all that was to happen to him thereafter.

He had learnt to write as well and, for the remainder of his life, he was never to be at a loss once he had pen and ink before him.

Meanwhile, his father, with a view to expanding the family income, had been spending the winter months with the navvies engaged in the Stelvio, Europe's highest Pass, which, rising from the Trafori Valley by a series of zig-zag bends, reaches an altitude of nine thousand feet. This was a laborious and never-ending task, with the Alpine winds blowing down and piling the drifts up almost as quickly as they were cleared.

Still a mere stripling, Joshua joined his father and became a navvy in his turn. His weekly wage, such as it was, he handed over, keeping back a few lire to buy a book or a magazine. On three evenings he attended the night school, where he learnt to speak and to read German.

When Saturday came round, they downed tools and went back to the Burat to be reunited with their family, and to fulfil the obligation of the Sunday Mass. In the disputes that arose between the workmen and their overseers, both father and son played the part of peace-makers, the one acting as a go-between, and the other, on occasion, boldly confronting the foreman and telling him just where he had to get off. One Saturday, the men were ordered to return, without fail, the following morning in order to put in an extra day's work. Joshua was up again, for the second time, like a jump-jack.

"We can't do that. It's Sunday and we have to go to Mass."

"There's no can't about it. I'm master here."

"No, you're mistaken. God's the master in this case. He comes first, you know."

"Very well! Have it your own way. I might have known how it would be with thirty-two millions of you imbeciles in Italy."

"Not thirty-two million, Sir. You're leaving yourself out. Say thirty-two millions and one."

The boy had learnt the Office of the Blessed Virgin by heart, and he was in the habit of reciting it during his work, to the amusement of his mates who tried, at first, to laugh him out of his flamboyant piety. But after the encounter with the foreman, the laughter was definitely off the bill of fare and, before long, Joshua had nearly everybody saying the Rosary.

There was a strong fibre of obstinacy in his character. Nothing could turn him aside from the routine of his religious duties, neither landslides nor avalanches. Saturday by Saturday, on his way home, he would drop into church to pay his respects to the Master referred to in his bout with the engineer-in-charge, and have a word, perhaps, with his priest who, by this time, was beginning to think that at least one of his parishioners had in him the makings of a saint. "Dear G," Don Angelo Rosatti wrote, "this is my first letter to you up there in the Stelvio. Your poor priest sends you his greetings and good wishes, just to encourage you in your work and in your fight for virtue. As to that, I pray you may be as immovable as the mountain peaks that surround you."

The day was approaching when Joshua was to leave the Pass and labour under a very different sky. But he never forgot these companions of his, the rough-and-ready men, some of them from distant parts, with whom he had shouldered the burden for so many years. There were no trade unions in those days ; and, amid the prevalent anti-clericalism of the early '90's, which saw a freemason elected Mayor of Rome, pressures were often brought to bear upon "those imbeciles," the working-class. Years later, addressing his brothers in a letter which, in due course, went the round of the Valley, he wrote :

"You must be men, nowadays, and must not allow yourselves to be imposed on against your will and your conscience. That's the only way to preserve your self-respect and win the respect of others. I found that out for myself, when I was twenty-five and working where you are."

As soon as he was old enough to have some confidence in himself, he joined forces with what was later to be known as Catholic Action, going quietly about the district looking up the families that had migrated in search of a living. A firm believer in a good Press, he described a man without a newspaper as no better than a monkey. The next thing, he was corresponding with the editor of the *Valtellina Courier*

here -

on the subject then agitating the country, the attempt being made in the Chamber of Deputies to legalise divorce. The working-class generally regarded this as a blow aimed at what little social security was left to them, the security of their own family life. Joshua took up the cudgels on behalf of those in his immediate circle, organizing protests and collecting signatures. The Masonic Lodges retaliated by calling the signatories "unpatriotic" and "a big bunch of ignorant fools." Then came the letter to the *Courier*, published on the morning of March 6th, 1903.

"These deputies, socialists and others, are all smiles as long as we workers are making money for them and allowing ourselves to be pushed around. But the moment we venture to open our mouths in protest against what we believe to be wrong and unjust, they change their tune and start calling us idiots and ignoramuses. We have at least had an elementary education and, therefore, can't be such dunces as all that. Lombardy is solidly against the measure, and there must be a few educated people in Lombardy. Silvio Pellico was against divorce, and who would dare to say that he was unpatriotic ?"

An apt enough citation, since, in the cause of Italian independence, Silvio Pellico had come near to being a martyr. Convicted on a trumped-up charge, he was condemned to death by the Austrians, the penalty being commuted to twenty years imprisonment with hard labour. He was released after eight years, but not before he had written the diary which was to electrify his countrymen, and is said to have done more harm to the Austrian cause than a defeat on the field of battle. *My Imprisonments* is a perfect thing of its kind, an unaffected and deeply moving account of his spiritual reactions to the sufferings he endured in the Austrian fortress. The passage in which he describes the spider which he taught to eat out of his hand is one of the most treasured pieces of Italian prose.

We can take it that Joshua was familiar with this book, and with Pellico's less known juvenile writings. The reference to him in the letter was certainly a clever move on the part of a navvy whose education never got beyond the third class in an elementary school : what chess-players would call a checkmate.

3

AFRICA CALLING

IF Joshua Dei Cas had little or no book-learning, in the strict sense, he had taste and opportunity for that without which the bookish man reads to small purpose. He was a great hand at wandering off on his own, in order to do some reflecting; heart-thinking, the Bible calls it, for want of which the land is made desolate, and maybe the mind as well. And now, when he felt himself to be getting on, his own future began to claim the attention of his secret thoughts. What was he going to do with his life? Were things to go on as they were, or would God, perhaps, rather have it otherwise? And, from then on, he kept asking for a bit of guidance in the matter.

Lord, what wilt thou have me to do?

Speak! for thy servant heareth.

We never can tell what may be waiting for us just round the corner. Some chance encounter, a few words dropped by accident within our hearing and, lo and behold! we are brought to a stand, and compelled to come to a decision altering the whole course of our life. A single scripture text converted Augustine, sent Anthony the Patriach of Monks into the desert, and Francis Xavier to the Far East. A book did the trick for Ignatius, and a Good Friday sermon for Angela of Foligno. We are going about our routine affairs, as usual, until one day there is a sudden and decisive intervention. Peter and Andrew, James and John had gone down to the same shore to the same boat a hundred times over; Saul had taken the road to Damascus more than once before: a day came when he and they did the usual thing once too often.

Joshua Dei Cas had been up to the Stelvio a hundred times over, going and returning by the same road. For years, he had been handling the same pick, the same shovel, the same everything. Then, one afternoon in a break between shifts, there was a sudden and decisive intervention in the shape of a bit of news.

"Joshua, shall I tell you something?"

"Yes, what is it?"

"A foreign missionary's coming to our place to give a lantern-lecture—all about Africa, Central Africa. He's just come back from there. He's a Verona Father."

"Is it possible?"

"Well, all I know is that our parish priest gave it out yesterday morning during Mass. At Oga, they're all excited about it. I dare say you'll be along, eh?"

Be along! He should just think so. And there was no difficulty about it, for Oga was a village quite close to Piatta. What a strange thing that this should have been sprung upon him, and he, of late, quite wrapped up in the pages of an illustrated magazine called *Nigrizia*, The Black People, published, at Verona, by the Verona Fathers. These missionary publications

$\longrightarrow$

The Dei Cas family. Brother Joshua second from the right, holding is favourite newspaper, with Teresina on his right and Riccardo on his left.

have multiplied since the first of them, the Annals of the Propagation of the Faith was issued in 1822, and it is safe to say that they have been responsible for scores of vocations, including that of Bishop Comboni himself, the founder of the Verona Fathers. It is known that a certain Lay-Brother in this very same Order, a native of the Trentino, was eating his bread and cheese by the side of the work he was engaged on, when he happened to glance at the paper his meal had been wrapped in. It contained an article on the subject of foreign missionary work and, there and then, he decided to devote the rest of his life to this service.

Joshua not only went along to the lecture, but he roped in as many others as he could lay hands on, so that the women might not have it all to themselves. It was a simple yet impressive affair. At the close, the bearded misionary, Father Tranquillo Silvestri, later to become Vicar Apoltolic of Khartum, made an earnest appeal to the young men in the audience to stir up the grace of God that was in them, and dedicate their lives to the cause of the Negro. They were our own brothers and sisters out there, made in the same imagine and likeness and redeemed by the same Precious Blood. The harvest was great, but the harvesters were all too few. Could any enterprise be more worthy of the attention and energy of a Christian! To carry the Good Tidings to those millions who, in so many ways, were the pathetic victims of their own errors and ignorances and, by so doing, to become one of the apostles? And, to put it at its lowest, didn't

←

Where Brother Joshua "muscled-in". The approach to the Stelvio, the highest pass in Europe reaching a level of over nine thousand feet. One of the zig-zag bends is in the foreground.

33

the white man owe some reparation to these same millions, some restitution for what had been taken from them ? It was not just a question of priests : lay-brothers were needed, able-bodied men in reasonably good health. What a field was waiting for their skills and their energy ! Without them the work could hardly go on.

This was true enough.

The lay-brothers in Religious Orders are no longer what they were. At one time there was hardly a monastic house, whether in town or country, without its complement of these workers who were cooks, tailors, sacristans, door-keepers and much else besides. Latterly, the shortage is such that women have had to be brought in as daily helps, and alterations made in the buildings for their accommodation.

But the Missionary Orders simply cannot afford these shortages. Men who have no call to be priests are required for the work of erecting and maintaining the mission-stations ; men like Martin Porres, who was a Jack of all Trades : masons, carpenters, electrical engineers, and mechanics of every kind. The Verona Fathers have always been fairly well supplied with these skilled men to whom are entrusted not just the odd jobs about the house, but substantial undertakings, as one can see for oneself when visiting hundreds of missions and schools and churches and hospitals in Africa, built by these same Brothers.

Before long we shall find Joshua busy sinking wells, organizing drainage-schemes and superintending the making of bricks, fifty thousand at a time, with himself the leading brick-maker. And, it is not only out in Africa or elsewhere. These same Fathers now have several establishments in England, and the cost of erecting these must have been halved thanks to their lay-brothers, some of whom are trained to become professional teachers and catechists.

*   *   *

The little sleep Joshua got the night following the lecture was punctuated by dreams and something like nightmares. There was he as large as life, apparently, and already under the merciless sun of the Dark Continent, being chased by lions and crocodiles, thanking God for the experience the Stelvio had given him in leaping over boulders and climbing precipices. He was up and on the job as usual the next day; but, during the breaks, he sat apart looking down into the Pass, where he seemed to see people with black skins moving about in the heat haze, among rows and rows of huts shaped like tents. And the noise the mountain torrents were making sounded, for all the world, like the voices of prisoners pleading for deliverance. That week was the longest ever, for he was aching to get back in order to unburden himself to his friend the parish priest.

Saturday came at last, after years of waiting, and the work's signal had hardly started before he was snatching at his pay-packet and making off by the shortest cut, strapping his knapsack about his shoulders as he ran along. Arrived at Piatta, he went first into the church and knelt down, tingling and breathing hard. Then he made for the presbytery and came straight to the point . . .

"You see, Father, I have really wanted to be a missionary since ever I remember, and last Sunday the lecture I heard at Oga settled the thing for me. How am I to go about it?"

"You want to begin to study at your time of life?"

"No! I want to be a lay-brother. According to the lecturer they are just as necessary. There are all sorts of things waiting for strong men to come and do them, buildings and farm-work; things that I am good at."

"Well, figliolo, patience. We shall see whether this is God calling or just someone imitating the sound of His voice."

When eventually that problem had been partly solved, another one cropped up.

"Have you spoken to your parents?"

"No, I haven't. I haven't had the courage. You tell them."

Nothing very surprising here. He was the eldest son, the hope of the family, and it was very plain to see that already the wear and tear was telling on his father. They would have to be told, of course, but wouldn't it be better to wait until he heard that the Verona Fathers were willing to have him? No use upsetting them before the time.

And so a whole year went by before the parish priest decided that, to put things off any longer, would be to fly in the face of divine providence.

"I tell you what, Joshua; write to Verona and state your case. If you like, you can pass the letter on to me and I can add a few words of my own. That will have to be done in any case, you know."

The letter was written and posted off. Then the applicant had a brain-wave. He would persuade his father to have a photograph taken, a family group. They might then begin to put two and two together, and that would soften the blow, in a way. In due course, the photograph was an accomplished fact. There it was, a fair specimen of the art as practised at that date, everyone stiff and rigid, and looking self-conscious probably for the first time in their life : the Father doing his best to play the part, the youngest with a medal round his neck, the Mother and her other children holding prayer-books in their hands, and Joshua in his shirt sleeves, a scythe on his shoulder, a spade at his feet and a newspaper between his fingers.

Those who have seen it for themselves tell us that there is no mistaking the prospective lay-brother— thick-set, somewhat bent about the shoulders, his merry good-humoured face ornamented by an untidy beard : that was one thing, at any rate, he was bringing ready-made to the missions.

A week later, the parish priest arrived at the house only to find that Anacleto was down with influenza. Would he excuse himself and call another time ? No, better take a header into the business and get it over.

"Has Joshua spoken to you ?"

"No ! Why ? What about ?"

"Well, to tell the truth, I have a letter here from the Superior of the African Missions notifying me that Joshua has been accepted as a lay-brother, and will be welcome in Verona at any time from today ?"

"Who did you say has been accepted ?"

"Joshua."

"Mamma Mia ! Not Joshua, surely !"

"Yes, Joshua. He has been wanting to go for the past twelve months and now it is all settled."

"A thunderbolt in a clear sky," to quote an account written some time ago. What could the Good God be thinking of to put such an idea into their son's head, and such a son ! It must be a mistake. It must be one of Joshua's usual pranks.

The culprit arrived back from the Stelvio the same evening, to find his mother in tears and, before long, he was mingling his own with hers. For the time being he could do little else, and he made some excuse and went off to his bedroom. That night there was hardly any rest for any of them. After the Sunday Mass there was a scene that is as old as the Gospel, with the correspondent of the *Valtellina Courier* using all his powers of persuasion, and the parents being at last won over to his point of view. It is no joke being a mother and a Catholic one at that, and his mother was the last to give in.

"You just can't imagine how I am feeling. But, if the Lord wants you, it is not for me to stand in your way. I can do nothing except give you my blessing."

The rest of the day was spent in saying good-bye to his friends and associates, and on Monday morning he heard Mass at 4.30 and received Holy Communion, packed a satchel with several loaves, a home-made cheese, and some clothing. He carried his fortune in his pocket—thirty lire. The stage-coach was at the door : he slipped upstairs and received his father's benediction on his knees. His parting words were :

"Never fear ! If I am not accepted into the Order, I shall know where the door of my home is all right."

His brother Ricardo ran after the coach until he could run no longer. Along the route, the village-folk lined up to wish him God-speed. And it was all over.

It is not easy to keep Manzoni out of a book of this kind, for he had the whole district at his finger-tips, and has described it as well as it will ever be described. Renzo and Agnes are embarking on the boat that is to carry them into exile.

"Farewell ! mountains springing from the waters and rising to the sky ; rugged peaks familiar to those who have grown up in their midst, and impressed upon their mind as clearly as the features of their nearest and dearest ; torrents whose varying tones can be picked out as easily as the voices of his own family : villages scattered white over the slopes like flocks of grazing sheep—farewell !"

The only difference this separation made in Joshua's interest in and affection for his family was to quicken the one and intensify the other. This he himself acknowledges in one of the many letters that were to find their way to the Valtellina during the next dozen years. Nor was the Valley ever far from his thoughts.

"Shall I ever see those places again, those beautiful mountains of ours ? One has to be in this part of Africa, which is as flat as a table from end to end, to appreciate them as one should. You there who live in Piatta, hold fast to your old church and steeple. If you only knew how people are living out here where there is neither church nor steeple."

4

IN THE WAKE OF AN APOSTLE

ALL honour to the explorers of Africa. But it in no way detracts from their heroism to recognise that, in certain parts of Africa, the trail had been blazed for them by the heroism of the Missionaries.

Livingstone's exploratory work has tended to obscure the fact that he was a delegate of the London Missionary Society and went into Africa primarily as an evangelist. As for the Sudan, Fathers Vinco, Knoblecher, Beltrame and many others made their way into that impenetrable region, and there they died, years before the expeditions identified with such names as Speke, Burton, or Baker. And there is this besides. These Missionaries ventured into the Dark Continent practically unattended, whereas the explorers were backed up by a personnel running to hundreds, sponsored by powerful organisations.

Father Angelo Vinco, who was responsible for bringing Daniel Comboni to Africa, went there himself in 1847, founded a mission station at Gondokoro, in Equatoria, as early as 1849 and died in 1854. When the explorers arrived among the Bari, they heard the natives singing the song of the SICK WHITE MAN, who refused to leave and go back to his country to get cured :

—Angelo, Angelo !
go back to Bellania :
for here is nothing but disease !
—No, no . . . I am quite at home here !
—Angelo, Angelo !
go back to Bellania,
where there are no mosquitoes !
—No, no . . . I am quite at home here ! . . .

Such was the heroism of the first Missionaries in the Sudan.

One of these Missionaries was Bishop Daniel Comboni himself, the founder of the Institute, to which Brother Joshua belonged, and of the Missionary Sisters, who take their name from the city of Verona.

Successively an Etruscan and a Gaulish centre, Verona or Veronia, as the Romans called it, was a flourishing city when London could have been nothing more than a river-settlement nestling on the slopes of the hill where St. Paul's now stands. The birthplace of Catullus, Vitruvius, Pliny the Elder, and the writer familiar to most budding latinists, Cornelius Nepos, its huge amphitheatre is in a better state of preservation than the Colosseum. The twelfth century cathedral is guarded by Charlemagne's two Paladins, Roland and Oliver. Situated at the cross-roads and astride the Adige, its strategic value was such that, in capturing it, the Goths considered themselves to be the masters of Italy.

Here, in 1867, Daniel Comboni, a native of Brescia, established the mother-house and training centre of his Institute of Missions to the Negroes, popularly known as the Verona Fathers. For years, the recruits for the Order were drawn almost exclusively from the neighbourhood and, even now, a surprising proportion of the members one comes across in England hail from northern Italy.

42

Comboni's concern for the Blacks amounted to a passion. "Either Africa or Death" was his motto from beginning to end. The determination to become a missionary came to him when, at the age of fifteen, he read an account of the Martyrs of Japan. His first Mass as a priest was a solemn dedication of his life to the service of the Africans. He was twenty-eight years of age when, with five companions, he reached the station of the Holy Cross more than a thousand miles up the Nile from Khartum. Within twelve months, two of the five priests had succumbed to fever, an ominous and constantly recurring indication of the hazards of such work, at a period when tropical diseases were hardly understood, and when the missionaries went into Central Africa equipped with little beyond their own heroism.

But Father Comboni did not give in. Before long he had published his *Plan for the Regeneration of Africa*, had founded his first missionary college at Verona, and was back in Africa organising his campaign. Five years later he took in hand the organisation of his Sisterhood—known in England as the Missionary Sisters of Verona—whose members have been, since then, a tower of strength to the Fathers with whom they collaborate in the various missionary fields.

One could not listen to his words and not be enthralled by them—and won over to his cause. He had a way of his own also in recruiting members for his Societies, going straight to the point as, for example, Giuseppa Scandola. As a result of a mission appeal made in a village church, she came to him with her mother in Verona. She was only a peasant girl, but she had plenty of apostolic spirit and one talent, at any rate, she was bringing to the common pool . . .

43

"What can you do ?" was Comboni's first question.

"I can make polenta," the girl replied.

"Oh well, that's fair enough. In the missions we need those who can do any or every kind of work." And with that Giuseppa was accepted. She had an idea, though, that she would like to say good-bye to her friends.

"Quite unnecessary," said Comboni, "that's something your mother can do for you."

To the convent, therefore, the new postulant went straight away, eventually reaching Africa where, during something like thirty years, she successfully negotiated quite a number of undertakings—not least, her own sanctification—over and above the cooking of polenta, and she happened to be the first Sister to work among the Shilluk, where Brother Joshua was to spend most of his missionary life.

Comboni had already toured the countries of Europe, including England, collecting funds. He made the acquaintance of the explorer Stanley and of General Gordon. In 1877 he was made Vicar Apostolic of Central Africa, with jurisdiction over Nubia, the Sudan and the territory south of the Lakes. He published a good deal of scientific matter, notably a geographical survey of Central Africa. As well as seven European languages, he could speak Arabic and seven negro dialects. On the eve of the Mahdist uprising, he sickened and died at the age of fifty, a victim of the bad climate of Khartum.

When Daniel Comboni was struggling to get Central Africa on to the missionary map, Italy at any rate was already familiar with the slogan : "Africa Converted by Africans," since it was an Italian Franciscan, Father Ludovico da Casoria, who was responsible for it.

Walking one day in the streets of Naples, he met two black boys accompanied by a priest. Then and there, he decided to respond to an inspiration which this encounter started up in his mind. He opened a school and the two boys were his first pupils. In the end, he had over sixty, all Blacks, and he set about training them to become missionaries in their own country.

Comboni had much the same conviction. No one knew better than he the difficulties confronting the European, however great his enterprise and his devotedness. He had had to stand by and see his most promising assistants falling, one by one, out of the ranks before ever their efforts were properly under way. Then there was the racial antagonism and, more especially, those political complications that have bedevilled missionary work nearly everywhere. The time was coming when this vital question was to form the subject of two Papal Encyclicals, but Bishop Comboni never lived to read them. He did, however, open in Cairo a house in which the new arrivals from Europe could stay for a period, and become acclimatised to their surroundings ; and, of course, then as now, the members of his Institute were obliged to have some knowledge of Arabic and of the native dialects.

Although the Institute itself has now about thirty native vocations and several seminaries in Africa itself, there was not much that the Bishop could do at that early stage. To all intents and purposes, he had only the one house at Verona, and the funds he had collected were barely sufficient to keep his struggling Order in being. As for a native seminary, that prospect was still a long way off.

The task of creating native priests is, for obvious reasons, an extremely arduous one, not to be carried through without careful consideration, well-laid plans and a long period of experimental training. The difficulties and obstacles confronting missionaries in Africa and elsewhere are hardly different from those obtaining in the world into which the Church was born; a society fermenting with pagan concepts and practices, and still quite uninfluenced by Christian ideals. St. Paul had his weather-eye very wide open when he was looking round for recruits.

"The man who is to be a bishop must be faultless, faithful to one wife, sober, discreet, modest, well-behaved, hospitable, experienced in teaching, no lover of wine or of brawling, courteous, neither quarrelsome nor grasping. He must be one who is a good head to his own family, and keeps his children in order by winning their respect: if a man has not learned how to manage his own household, will he know how to govern God's Church? *He must not be a new convert,* or he may be carried away by vanity. He must bear a good character, too, in the world's eyes or he may fall into disrepute. Deacons, in the same way, must be men of decent behaviour, men of their word, not given to deep drinking or to money-getting, keeping true to the faith. These, in their turn, must first undergo probation and be only allowed to serve if no charge is brought against them . . ."

During the nineteenth century, several attempts were made to create an indigenous clergy. Most of them ended in disaster. It was not until 1886 that converts among the Polynesians could be advanced to the altar with any hope of success. It was not until 1893 that a seminary for all India was opened in Ceylon. According to statistics published in 1950, there were, at that date, eleven thousand natives already ordained with about eighteen thousand undergoing their training. But in Bishop Comboni's time, such a state of affairs was only a thing to be dreamt about.

At the time of writing (1962), his Institute has over fourteen hundred members established in a dozen countries. The main centres of their operations are in the Sudan, in Uganda, Canada, Switzerland, Egypt, Mozambique, Brazil, Ecuador, Mexico and the United States. About a hundred youths, from all parts of the British Isles, are being trained as priests and lay-brothers in colleges in England.

But when Joshua Dei Cas was on his way to present himself as a candidate, the enterprise was still in its first period of growth ; and, apart from a small foundation in Rome and another equally small in Brescia, the house in Verona was still the sole establishment and served for all purposes. It was situated in the Viccolo Pozzo not far from the Mayoral palace, and the eleventh century church of St. Zeno, who was a contemporary of Julian the Apostate and of St. Ambrose. It was the wall surrounding this mother-house that was scaled by the intrepid man from the mountains.

Within a matter of hours, he had settled down and was feeling very much at home. No doubt, he imagined that now all communication with his family would be cut off or, at any rate, reduced to a mere trickle. He was mistaken, though ; for one of the first things he was told to do, as a matter of obedience, was to write home, to write at once and to write regularly. Whatever renunciations were in store, correspondence, apparently, was not going to be one of them. This was an agreeable surprise. The next discovery he made was that daily prayers for the spiritual and temporal welfare of those belonging to them, were part and parcel of the devotional routine of the community. That tit-bit of information he proceeded to pass on to those he had left behind in the Burat.

"There are a good fifty of us here, Fathers and Brothers, some of whom are just back from Africa where, please God, I myself shall soon be doing my bit. One thing, my affection for you all is stronger than ever ; and, as for forgetting you, it is impossible here, because in the manual they have given me, I find that there are prayers said every day for our parents, relations, friends and enemies. Another thing, I am even closer to heaven now than when I was at work in the Stelvio Pass ; although, mind you, you mustn't run away with the idea that, in order to get there, you have to do what I've done. Nothing of the sort ! If God comes first, it's all the same wherever you are.

"As for you, Mother, I hope you won't be annoyed when I tell you that I've found another mother down here who is a great help to me. She has a grotto in the corner of our garden and, before recreation, we all get together round her statute, and ask her to keep us up to the scratch."

We may be thankful that, from the beginning, his superiors not only left him free but encouraged him to write. And write he did without intermission right up to the week before his death. Simple, informative letters they are, calculated to give real pleasure since, in them, the accent is always on those at the receiving

➤

Brick-making in progrss, showing a native hut and the primitive transport. The wheel was first brought to this part of the Sudan by the Verona Fathers.

48

end. If the art of letter-writing consists in carrying on a conversation on paper, then he had the touch of the artist : something of an achievement, when we consider that he had made little or no contact with book-learning and was, from first to last, occupied with the kind of labour that normally makes even the handling of a pen irksome if not impossible.

Stilus virum arguit. Doctor Johnson was not inclined to accept this, because "very few can boast of hearts which they dare lay open to themselves : and, certainly, what we hide from ourselves, we do not show to our friends."

If we are to believe those who are in a position to know, those who were in touch with Joshua Dei Cas for years, he was at least one exception to this general rule, if general rule it be. Better than any photograph, better perhaps than any biography, however painstaking, the letters are the man himself without any possibility of doubt, a self-portrait from the life.

Altogether they constitute a legacy to his brethren, bequeathed by one who had nothing else to leave. And they are of value to the public at large, especially to those who are burdened by the trials and tribulations of this life. Many of them were sent off when the writer was in the last stages of the disease, although one would never suspect it, going by the letters themselves. And that in itself is heartening. Here is one with no social pretensions, no educational advantages, living and dying in a foreign land surrounded by

←

A Missionary group photographed on the spot. Brother Joshua, heavily bearded, in the rear centre, with six Verona Fathers and Brothers as well as native converts.

lepers and a leper himself, bereft of those comforts and conveniences which we can hardly imagine ourselves being without : and yet, he never falters, never bemoans his fate, and the letters are genuine and upstanding like the man himself.

There might be little enough in the attaché-case which he carried to Verona, but his ready-made equipment was considerable, and it was well-seasoned. He was used to privations and discomforts. He had been brought up the hard way by those who had no softness or nonsense about them. For him, as for many a one who joins a Religious Order, the vow of poverty was going to mean that he was much better off than when he was at home : well fed, well clothed, well shod and well housed.

It takes all sorts to make a community, even a religious community, and one hardship of the monastic life is that you are obliged to live, work and play with companions not of your own choosing. In the world, being "good company" or a "good mixer" may mean no more than this that, having made a careful selection, you are disposed to be free and easy with those you fancy ; and, of course, you can always cold-shoulder an acquaintance who gets on your nerves.

It is otherwise in the cloister. But Joshua's nerves had been toughened by years and years of compulsory contact with a varied assortment of working men, some of them difficult to get on with, and all of them under the strain of a difficult and irksome job. You could hardly say he was entering the novitiate with kid gloves on his hands and patent-leathers on his feet.

For the next fifteen years or so, these same hands and feet were never to be idle, and it was on the former that the first symptoms of the leprosy appeared. A labourer, that was what he had been, and that was what he was to remain until health and strength gave out. But, early on, up in the Stelvio Pass, this worker had discovered the religious significance of work, had made it part of his religion, no matter what the work might be; and, in this way, had found out for himself that every common act of ours has, or can be made to have, a sacramental character, can become the outward sign of an inward grace.

And you could scarcely say that he was, so far, only on the lower rungs of the ladder of perfection. He knew how to pray and how to meditate. He had had a long and unbroken experience of the interior life. His reverence for the Church, for those in authority in it and with everything appertaining to it was unquestioned. He had a lot to learn, no doubt, but the foundations were already in, and the superstructure itself only needed pointing and smoothing down.

The usual procedure in Religious Orders is for the candidate to be put through his paces for a spell as a postulant, before being clothed in the habit and taking his place as a fully-fledged novice. This procedure was not followed in Joshua's case. He passed through the novitiate, indeed, but when he left it and went to Africa, he was still a postulant dressed in his ordinary clothes. He remained like that for fourteen years.

"You ask me," he wrote to his family, "how the clothing ceremony is carried out. Well, it won't affect me for a while yet. I have to wait. What's the odds! Being here is the main thing, and it is very good of them to let me stay at all."

The Superior General couldn't make up his mind. There was no question as to his goodness and spiritual aptitudes. There was no question as to his ability, and his willingness to work and to work hard. In this matter, it was the rein he needed rather than the spur. Thanks to the practice he had had up in the Pass, he was wont to take a flying-leap at each and any task that offered, without even waiting for the word Go.

At the same time, there was that about him that needed some sorting out, a certain uncouthness of manner, a general ungainliness. He was awkward in a room, awkward at table, this navvy who had, for so long, roughed it in rough places, with rough workmates. He has told us himself that, in his own home, he ate his food sitting on a box : in the Stelvio Pass it would be on a boulder. Accustomed to the thrust and parry of working men everywhere, his talk was staccato and savouring of flippancy. Going round with his mouth half open, with a surprised look on his face, he could easily have been mistaken and was, in fact, mistaken for a person of low-grade intelligence. He looked ill-at-ease in his good clothes.

These external traits of character might be misleading. Doctor Johnson could be uncouth to the verge of savagery. Oliver Goldsmith often looked and felt like a fool ; and, on his own confession, so sometimes did Cardinal Newman who, incidentally, made a poor show at dressing up, and a poor show at a big function like the opening of a certain church, for instance, when he was Deacon and astonished the rubricians.

In the matter of his high spirits and his partiality for practical jokes, he had some quite respectable saints on his side : Francis of Assisi, who was not averse to play-acting on occasion, and Philip Neri, who played tricks on everybody not excepting Cardinals.

All very well. But in the foreign missionary field the personnel has to be on its guard. This or that which might pass muster in a Catholic country would be dangerous among natives, whose reactions to any sort of unseemly behaviour in their teachers are apt to be swift and unfavourable. And this was especially the case in the Africa at that period, where opposition to the missionary was still strong, particularly among the chiefs, who were only too eager to seize on anything that might help to discredit them.

While things were in this undecided state, Father Frederigo Vianello entered on his duties as Novice Master, a sensible priest with some insight into the complexities of the human character, and with a genuine regard for those committed to his charge, young men who, like the Apostles, had left everything they prized in order to answer the call, and were now, at the most generous and confiding stage of their life, handing themselves over, lock, stock and barrel, to those entrusted with their formation.

What goes on in the novitiate of a Religious Order is not publicised, with the result that the outside world has nothing to go by except guess-work, and the guesses are usually wide of the mark. A novitiate is a period of initiation, and the word initiation may convey the idea of a course of shock-treatment designed to see how much the nerves of the subject can stand; a remorseless psychological pounding and pommelling persisted in for twelve months. Failing that, the house of novices is thought of as a kind of barrack-square, in which raw recruits are put through their paces at the bidding of an angry and hoarse-voiced drill-sergeant, until the paces have become instinctive and mechanical.

Were tactics of this kind to be employed, the result

for Religious Orders themselves would be suicidal, calculated as they are to produce neurotics or deserters from the ranks.

The subject has to be disciplined to a sustained routine of external observances. But these are the tools of the trade, so to say, the mechanics of the business. Gestures and formulas, made and pronounced with precision, are means to an end. Were they treated as ends in themselves, the image or appearance would be substituted for the reality, and the living person displaced by the machine, a well-oiled machine that can be relied on to give every satisfaction—as a machine. Affected attitudes and postures, sham humility, sham simplicity, sham obedience are to be expected and are appropriate on the stage, but they just will not do in the domain of religion.

"Quench not the Spirit," that has to be the ruling principle all the way through : "What God has joined together let no man put asunder." Interiorization : that is the objective. Nothing will compensate for weakness at the centre : muscles developed at the expense of the heart. And since the personality of the subject is the abiding dwelling-place of the Spirit, Novice Masters know that that has to be respected as well, otherwise the personality stands a chance of being reduced to the mere ghost of itself. Brow-beating and ridicule are dangerous weapons, and constant use can turn them into lethal weapons.

Father Vianello was fully alive to the responsibilities of his office. It did not take him long to discover the goodness and generosity lying underneath the rough exterior of the navvy from the Valtellina, and he acted accordingly. Perhaps he had the Curé of Ars in mind, whose appearance and "goings on" got on the nerves of his fellow-clergy, but who was, for all that, defended and commended by the Archbishop of Lyons : "Gentlemen, believe me, we could all do with some of Monsieur Vianney's simplicity."

Joshua, therefore, was not sent home. "Let him have a trial, a long trial if necessary. Let him go to Africa as a lay-co-operator. It's my belief that the day will come when the whole Institute will rejoice to see him wearing the habit": that was probably how the Novice Master felt about it.

And so the new postulant fell into line with the Order of the Day. The community rose at five, meditated for an hour, and heard or said Mass. After breakfast, there was work until mid-day when there was the usual examination of conscience followed by dinner. Recreation lasted for an hour and, in summer, there was the siesta. Work then went on until six : there was a visit to the Blessed Sacrament, spiritual reading and supper, with recreation, night prayers and so to bed. In the case of the novices, this programme was somewhat amplified. From time to time, as a diversion, Rengo came along to break the silence of the cloister, Rengo being the great bell of the Municipality calling the Conscript Fathers into full session.

At the end of sixteen months Joshua was told to get ready for Africa. He dashed off a letter to the Burat :

"I am going ; Today I knelt at the Superior's feet promising obedience until death, and I'll keep my promise even if the world tumbles about my ears."

He was not allowed to spend the customary few days with his family, and he wasn't sorry : it would only mean another painful separation and more tears. He and the friend accompanying him arrived in Venice after a three hours run and, at midnight, they embarked for Trieste.

"My ancestors were here for years serving in the Austrian army and here am I enrolled in a very different service."

Five days after leaving Brindisi, they were in Alexandria, whence they pushed on to Cairo and the south.

———————

5
AMONG THE SHILLUK

ON his arrival in Egypt, that land of surprises, Joshua had a number of surprises of his own to write home about.

"At the railway station, what do you think I saw? A youth saying his rosary : beads something like ours only with no crucifix. Anyone doing this in a waiting room in Italy would be likely to make some people laugh : here no one pays any attention to it . . . Then, in Cairo, when I was out with one of our Brothers, a funeral procession came by with a blind man among the mourners. And the Brother up and tells me that this man had been to Mecca, and had put his eyes out in honour of Mahomet."

The custom of using a string of beads for praying purposes is not, of course, confined to Catholics, nor yet to Mohammedans and Catholics ; but the Moslem rosary which, at first sight, looks rather like ours, consists of ninety-nine beads, each bead representing one of the attributes of God which, according to the Koran, number one short of a hundred. As these pass through the fingers of the Arab, he meditates on or directs his mind to the attribute indicated by the bead.

Evidently Egypt, even now, had one foot in the other world, with something of the ancient religious earnestness still surviving, though in a different form; that pertinacity with which its people once wrestled with the eternal problem of immortality. Not all the links connecting the past and the present were broken. Cairo was standing there on the site of Memphis whose founder, Menes, was the first known king ever to rule over the Nile Valley; and, in its neighbourhood, Cheops erected the first pyramid. Farther north was Heliopolis to which Plato came for instruction and, before him, Moses, in order to acquire "all the learning of the Egyptians."

After a short rest, the little party set off for Khartum, passing through the Thebaid where Paul was born, "the Most Illustrious and Constant of all Anchorites," where the first monks swarmed like bees; passing Karnak, a museum in itself, with a temple two thousand feet long and columns some of which are thirty-six feet in circumference; passing the Valley of the Kings, traversing the district where, according to the ancient boast, the pure Egyptians, "Ramses People," lived. It was a twenty hours journey terminating at Asswan hard by Elephantine Island, "the last outpost of civilisation," where the ancients had their first sight of the African elephant in its wild state and surroundings.

A fortnight later, they were in Khartum, where the White Nile and the Blue Nile join forces, and travel together to Cairo and the open sea: a journey of three thousand four hundred miles all told. Khartum, where General Gordon had met his death not long before, was the capital of the Anglo-Egyptian portion of the Sudan.

Bilad-el-Sudan, that is to say, the Country of the Blacks, covers nearly a million square miles, being hemmed in, in the north by Egypt and the Desert of

Libya, by Kenya in the south, in the east and west by the Red Sea, Eritrea and Abyssinia, and by French Equatorial Africa respectively. It was colonized by the Egyptians round about 2000 B.C. But the day came when the Sudanese retaliated by invading Egypt, conquering it and establishing a dynasty which lasted until the Assyrians swept it away. In the Sudan itself, there were two kingdoms, one overthrown by the Romans in 23 B.C., the other by the Abyssinians in A.D. 350.

Christian missionaries from Constantinople evangelised the country early on, the fruits of their labours surviving for eight hundred years, when they were engulfed by the rising tide of Mohammedanism. After that, there was chaos and civil war, paving the way for the Egyptian invasion in 1821. The new masters did little for the Sudan beyond collecting taxes, and conveying the natives to the great slave-market at Khartum. For the Sudanese, things went from bad to worse, until the battle of Omdurman, in 1898, led to the setting up of a joint-administration by Egypt and England, pledging itself to the primary task of promoting the welfare and vindicating the rights of the inhabitants.

Peace gave the missionaries their opportunity and they soon began to avail themselves of it. Bishop Comboni was not the pioneer, but there is no doubt that his exertions on behalf of this territory, cut short by his early death, facilitated the efforts of all those coming after him. Since 1846, the Sudan had formed part of the Vicariate of Central Africa, taking in Egypt south of Asswan, Uganda and the district adjoining Lake Tchad; and now, at the end of the nineteenth century, the task of evangelising the territory, interrupted by the Mahdist rising, was taken up in earnest. The Verona Fathers opened a house of their Order and worked alongside a similar missionary body with headquarters at Brixen. Their efforts were limited to the negro tribes of which the Shilluk were the most powerful and widely-spread.

Several months later, the news reached the Valtellina.

"From Khartum we went far up the Nile until we reached Tonga, the most beautiful place in the world !"

This description does not quite correspond with the impression of tourists and explorers. Tonga is situated at the mouth of the Bahr-el-Ziraf, the Giraffe River. Its only attraction lay in the fact that it was densely populated, and so provided the missionaries with a favourable field for their operations. In itself, it was as much swamps as anything else, extensive marshes infested by mosquitoes. It is on record that the mere sound of the name brought a curse to the lips of every boatman plying on the Nile who heard it.

The Shilluk were here in force, a proud and resolute people, suspicious of foreigners to the verge of hatred, a hatred kept alive by the memory of the desperate battles they had fought to protect their families from the raids of the Arab slave-traders. Joshua Dei Cas was to work here, alongside his brethren, for fifteen years : spade-work it proved to be, since it was not only a question of making the mission-station habitable, but of preparing the minds of the tribesmen for the reception of the faith. From the start, he had a real affection for these natives who, for all their understandable hostility, were affable and good-natured at heart. They, in their turn, developed so strong a liking for him that, by the time he had to pack up and leave Tonga, they were eating out of his hand.

The Shilluk kingdom is a ribbon grass-land about one hundred and fifty miles in length, dotted with small villages of some twenty or thirty families. These centres of population are, for the greater part, situated close to the Nile, but far enough away to escape the inundations of that extraordinary river. In the dry season, when the water-holes are empty, they are or were completely dependent on it, and the women-folk had to trudge as much as ten miles, there and back, and do it every day, in order to keep their supply going. The soil and the river between them provide them with food ; millet, ground and baked, is the chief article of diet.

Cattle raising is a matter of necessity for more reasons than one. No marriage can take place until at least ten head of cattle have been paid over to the father of the prospective bride. Where the hire-purchase system operates, the young wife can be taken from her husband should the payments fall into arrears. The result of this strictly-observed custom is that polygamy is the exception rather than the rule ; for, apart from the big chiefs, very few are well enough off to be able to afford more than one wife, that is to say, more than ten cows. The married woman is regarded as a piece of property, so that, when her husband dies, she is handed over to the next-of-kin along with the furniture.

For all their errors and superstitions, the Shilluk, like the Africans generally, are essentially a religious people, firm believers in a God who is the Creator and Lord of all, the Master of life and death. Out and out idolatry has turned out to be less common than was thought years ago, when research into the subject was apt to be superficial ; and, taking the word in its wider sense, it may be that quite a fair amount of it is to be found in our own midst.

On entering and leaving a Shilluk village, you are greeted exactly as you might be if you were dealing with pious Christians : "God has brought you"; "May God guard you." *Omnia exeunt in mysterium*—on that point the natives are in no kind of doubt. Behind everything about them, including their own lives, lies the mystery of the eternal and divine. And this mystery is to be feared, reverenced and respected. Somewhat after the manner of the Israelites of old who said : "Don't let God speak to us : you do it instead," they offer no sacrifices and no public worship to Jwak-Atang, the All Highest and the Unapproachable. All their ceremonies are directed to the traditional hero of their race, a kind of Moses, who led them from the Great Lakes of Uganda into their present abode. This captain has the status of a Saviour and a Mediator and his shrines are to be found everywhere. The medicine men make up the only thing resembling a priesthood with which they are familiar. On all great occasions, animals are sacrificed to the Mediator, Nyi Kang.

Important people in the community, beginning with the king, are not allowed to die a natural death, but are smothered when it is seen that they have no chance of recovering. This would apply to old people as well, and to those suffering from a painful disease. It is considered a disgrace to die naturally. They believe in a short of Purgatory after death, a long and painful journey which the soul must undertake before arriving at its destination. From time to time, the deceased are commemorated by means of ceremonial dances followed by a feast.

About certain matters, they appear to be more sensitive than we are, certainly more vindictive. If a charge is made by one party and denied by the other, the man and the woman concerned are taken to the river and thrown in, as soon as a crocodile appears, and it is left to his superior sagacity to determine on which side the truth lies. Cannibalism is still practised on the quiet, and fifty years ago it was sometimes dangerous to accept an invitation to dinner, since you yourself might end up on the menu as the *chef d'oeuvre*.

Under the influence of the missionaries, these customs have been gradually losing their hold; but, even yet, nothing short of a direct appeal to the king is able to prevent this or that cruelty or injustice being perpetrated.

The Christian faith was brought to the Shilluk tribe, in the first instance, by an Italian Lazarist, Father Mansori, who came to Khartum after being expelled from Abyssinia, and opened a mission-station. This was in 1842. Fifteen years later, some missionaries from Italy, among them Daniel Comboni, the founder of the Verona Fathers, came into the territory and made a start. But it was not until 1871 that any real progress was made. Even then there were grievous setbacks. Comboni died, the Sudan was desolated by a famine, the Mahdist revolt broke out, which meant that the

→

Dentistry "de luxe & al fresco". The painless extractor is Hakim (Doctor) Brother Poloniato to you, the same who discovered Joshua Dei Cas on the doorstep of the Verona Monastery.

personnel of the missions were thrown into goal, remaining prisoners at Omdurman for ten years.

With the suppression of the revolt, things moved rapidly. In 1900 a station was opened at Lul and later at Tonga and Detwok ; the three places identified with the activities and the heroic sacrifice of Joshua Dei Cas.

───────

←

Teresina Dei Cas, the Wise Woman and well-loved sister who watched over Brother Joshua's career like a Guardian Angel and was the recipient of most of his letters.

6
SO MUCH ONE MAN CAN DO

THE Romans may not have prayed to Father Tiber, as Macaulay suggested, and Kublai Khan's sacred river running down to the sunlit sea may have had its source in Coleridge's imagination. All the same, rivers, especially big rivers, have had a religious character from time immemorial.

As for the Nile, that had a priesthood of its own, and the Egyptians regarded its behaviour as an act of God's special providence. The Coptic liturgy of St. Mark contains a prayer asking the Almighty to "raise the waters to their due level." The Nile was what it was called, the Food of Egypt ; and, among the punishments which the prophet Isaiah predicted for its people, was the treachery of the river : "The streams of the bank shall be dried up."

But equally disastrous might be the periodic rising of the Nile beyond its customary level. This happened more than once in ancient times, the phenomenon being duly noted on the inscriptions. From these we learn that, forty-four centuries ago, the rise was twenty-seven feet above anything recorded since ; and we also learn that the average rise at that period was twelve feet above the average in modern times.

For this reason, the group of villages known as

Tonga was sited well back from the river, and on rising ground which checked the inundations. But the land in between the villages and the river was a vast swamp which made the settlement almost inaccessible in the rainy season. The first thing needing to be done was the erection of a dam high enough and wide enough to keep the water at bay, and give the swamp a chance of drying up. Joshua took charge of this operation, coaxed a number of the natives on to the job and, in spite of the blistering sun and the blistering insects, had the thing finished in three months.

Then, if they were to survive, they had to make sure of a supply of good drinking-water. Sunken wells were unheard of in the district; and, with the superstitious dread of the unknown by which we are all more or less infected, the Shilluk refused to have anything to do with the sinking of this one. Their forefathers had found the Nile water good enough, and there was no necessity for such innovations. But, in its course, the river here passes over great tracts of decaying vegetable matter, so that Europeans can neither willingly drink its water nor stomach it when drunk. The missionaries, therefore, had to tackle the thing themselves; and, presently, the natives who had been astonished at seeing the digging going down sixty feet, were astonished again when they saw fresh water being brought sixty feet to the surface.

Started only a short time before, the mission, so far, had neither a decent church nor a decent house, only a few improvised huts made of wood and straw. Having solved the water problem, attention was turned to the buildings, with Joshua in the forefront of the enterprise. As an inducement to the natives to lend a hand, he would roll up his trouser-legs and go bare-footed into the ditches to tread the mud which, apparently, had to be well kneaded, like the dough of a loaf. It had to be washed as well and then dried, and carried to the oven at the right moment; otherwise, all the labour was in vain.

For the fire and the moulds wood was needed, and this had to be carted from the distant forest in its raw state, seasoned in the sun, and then cut into the proper lengths. There were plenty of discouragements and set-backs. There was even a strike; for, just while everything was in full swing, the drums began to beat as a warning to the natives that a hippopotamus hunt was starting, the equivalent of a "down-tools," which left the four missionaries to get on with the job by themselves.

Nevertheless Joshua was soon sending home another bulletin.

"In the past few days, we have made six hundred thousand bricks with the help of the Negroes who, I may say, have to be watched all the time; if you take your eyes off them, the work has to be done all over again."

One can only suppose that these natives, domiciled in thatched wooden huts, had never had any occasion to learn this art or craft, which must be among the oldest in the world, going back, as it does, far beyond anything done by the Egyptians or Chaldeans.

> "And each one said to his neighbour,
> come, let us make bricks and bake
> them with fire, and let us make a tower
> the top whereof may reach to heaven."

It was not the want of mud, since the river was never very far away. Nor need kilns have worried them, not with the kind of sun they were used to.

The walls of Babylon were built partly with burned, and partly with unburned bricks.

After the brick-making, the thatching : a skilful operation which the natives, through long practice, can carry out with their eyes shut. The millet, which is a staple article of their diet, is sown in July without any preliminary ploughing, hoeing or manuring. The plants can spring up to as much as ten feet. In the autumn, the ears are pulled off, laid out on tables to be dried and then carried to the villages by the women. Early in the new year, when the stalks have been hardened by the heat, they are cut down, and the thatchers set to work on the houses which need re-roofing, or on such new huts as have just been built. These workers are paid for their labour in beer, great quantities of which are brewed for the purpose.

"You will be pleased to hear that our house is going up, two floors with eight rooms in each, and divided by a corridor. One room is set aside as a chapel, but by the new year we shall start on a church, twenty metres long ; and, if the devil doesn't butt in with his horns, it will be ready before the rainy season. I am the only Brother left now, as the other has been sent to another station ; and, since Yours Truly is no good at making altars and church-fittings, the two Fathers have to do this part of the work."

A kitchen was badly needed as well, but it had to wait. All they had, in the meantime, was a lean-to shed with a steel roof which the hot sun converted into an oven. In this, Joshua the cook, worked away without complaining, thankful that its position outside made it possible for him to keep in touch with his Blacks, and do a bit of instructing while the pots were boiling. Food was not plentiful and sometimes ran short. The flour had to be brought from Khartum, and keeping it from going sour was a problem. Bred up in a home where every penny had to be accounted for, our cook had a horror of wastefulness, and watched over the goods of the community as a mother watches over her child.

Small need to say that our friend was in his element. For him, all this was just the thing, well within the compass of his skill and his energy. Dams and wells, and now a canal. In April and May the level of the Nile drops, leaving the surrounding land at the mercy of the summer heats which ruin everything that has been planted. Nothing would save the situation except a deep channel, long enough to prevent the water from draining off, and of a width sufficient for purposes of irrigation. This one was, in fact, six hundred metres long and, when it was finished, the produce of the fields was able to thrive and multiply. And such produce : bananas, oranges, lemons, sweet potatoes, sugar canes, chicory, peas, runner beans, tomatoes, pepper-grass and lettuces, especially lettuces about which Joshua wrote an enthusiastic letter to his family.

True, the crickets and flies had still to be reckoned with, and the locusts who, if and when they chanced to come, swept the board clean. But that, one could do nothing about, because once properly started a swarm of the pests is very difficult to check, even with modern appliances. The only practical thing is to destroy the eggs in the hatching-grounds. Grass-land adjoining sand is very susceptible to their inroads ; which probably accounts for their appearance at Tonga, where the visitations would, no doubt, be on a small scale, unlike those in the Red Sea area, one of which was estimated to be two thousand square miles in extent.

When all else failed, Joshua would take his gun or his rod and do some hunting or fishing. From these expeditions, he might come back soaking wet; but, as he said, there was no need to change; the sun saw to that.

So much can one man do
If he but act and know.

No mistake, he had a way with him, and before long it began to tell. His very status as a layman was an advantage. He could mix freely among the Shilluk, give them a hand with their work, or advise them on how to go about it. And he usually had something in his pockets, a few lemons and greens, and the small pepper plants which were greatly coveted in those parts. He was their friend all right; there was no doubt about that: and, when he made his appearance, he would be surrounded by a dancing crowd and escorted in state to the village.

He had been roughing it all his life; and that was another advantage. Fastidiousness was a word he did not know the meaning of; and it is this same fastidiousness that sometimes creates a barrier between us and the objects of our compassion. "I wouldn't mind, if they were not so dirty, if they were not so repulsive, if they were not so dishonest, if they were not such liars." And the dirt and the repulsiveness and the dishonesty and lying act like acid on one's charity, testing its strength and, only too often, burning it away.

It is so easy to forget that destitution, beside making short work of the proprieties, can render the practice of the virtues extremely difficult. According to the legend, Abraham turned a beggar adrift because of his bad manners, and was rebuked by the Almighty for his pains.

Outside the house and inside, the Blacks swarmed about the *Abuna*, as they insisted on calling him, although he was not even a Brother never mind a Father. They came bringing their complaints and grumbles, their sores and their disfigurements, sometimes their rudeness. Joshua never turned a hair, it seems, and it probably cost him nothing in the way of self-restraint and self-control to bid them welcome. He had never had anything remotely resembling a drawing-room unbringing. He jokes away, in his letters, about the forthright descriptions of their symptoms which he had to listen to ; he, meanwhile, looking very sage and being equally forthright in his recommendations. Before his arrival, the virtues of castor oil were unknown to the Shilluk. Before he left them, there was hardly a man, woman or child that was not prepared to swear by that magic remedy ; with definite qualifications, we may suppose.

There was a certain amount of pilfering as well, and he dealt with it in his own characteristic way : that old woman, for instance, a near relation of those who prowl around the Self-Service stores, servicing themselves at the expense of the stores. Joshua could not make out why his hens had stopped laying. But he had his suspicions and was on the look out. Enter the old woman (applause).

"Abuna, I have no salt. Will you give me some ?"

"Listen, Mamma Maya, we ourselves are short of salt just now. And we are short of eggs. I tell you what, if you bring me some eggs, I will give you salt in exchange."

"Very well, Abuna."

That evening Joshua went to the hen-house and marked the eggs with a pencil. For the time being, at any rate, he was an *agent provocateur*.

Scene 2.

"Here are the eggs, Abuna."

"Good morning, Mamma. Have you slept well ?"

"Yes, may God protect you ! Here are the eggs, I say."

"Yes, yes : let me see if they are fresh. Watch ! I break them one by one . . . No, they are not fresh. They are bad as I thought, very bad eggs. And, now shall I tell you why they are bad eggs ? . . . Listen, Maya, you must never do it again, because the Lord does not like it. But, do not be afraid, I will give you the salt all the same."

Then the trials came one after another, malaria first of all, henceforward a regular visitor. "No one need die of malaria": so we have been assured lately on the highest authority. Yet, this is still the biggest health problem confronting the tropics. It is estimated that anything up to half a million African children die of it every year, because of the lack of medical services. At the beginning of the century, the missionaries were already provided with safeguards, but these did not stop it from coming. Our letter-writer reports :

"From time to time, we go down with it for a week or so, and get up only to catch it again : after a month or so. The fever isn't dangerous, but it is very persistent."

Then came the news that Ricardo, the young brother who had run after the coach when Joshua left Piatta, had passed away.

"When I left you, I felt certain that I would find you all in your usual places on my return . . . Let us accept

74

the will of God. Ricardo was, if I may say so, the heir of my thoughts. On the Sunday I left, he confided his difficulties to me and his hopes, matters which brothers usually keep from one another. But have courage! Try even to be happy about it, if that is possible for you."

His father's health had been causing great anxiety for some time.

"How I wish that I could be ill in your place! Let us pluck up our courage: the cross is the inheritance of man, especially of those predestined to eternal glory. Our time on earth is very short, and our troubles will soon be over. Our misfortunes are great no doubt, but then they could be far greater. Let me send you this prescription which was given to me at Verona, and which I have tried with great success: Take each day as it comes and think as little as possible about the future. We don't in the least know what God may do for us tomorrow."

But, twelve months later, Anacleto was called to his reward, and another letter speaks feelingly of the days when the two worked side by side in the Stelvio. He could only remind them that the head of the house had sacrificed himself for his family, and was surely entitled to his rest.

"Dry your tears: weeping is only for sins. I can't give him back to you, so you must wait for God to do it in his own time."

Still, there was plenty to distract his mind. A priest came from Khartum to give the community the spiritual exercises known as a Retreat. What with one thing and another, the papyrus reeds chiefly, the boat due to take him back was delayed for several days, and the Father was getting restive. Joshua told him to go to bed as usual, and keep his clothes on. "I'll be on the look-out and I'll give you a call." One night at 2 a.m. the siren sounded from the river and the sleeper was roused. But there had been some flooding in the interval, and the way was barred by a fairly deep swamp.

"Father, I'm used to heavy loads. Up with you on my back, and I'll get you through in a jiffy."

There was no room in the boat, as it happened, so the two had to face about and recross the swamp as before, and wait for the arrival of the next vessel, five days later, when Operation Pick-a-Back was repeated for the second time running.

To cheer him, there came from his sister Teresina some views of the district around his old home. After thanking her, he went on :

"Don't worry about me. I shall be content to die here ; and, between ourselves, it may be soon because, you know, pumpkins mature quickly in this climate. Will you be surprised if I tell you that I am already as bald as our father was at 60."

Next, he was sent to Khartum for a rest and change of air, and after two and a half months he came back to Tonga, refreshed in body and soul. In the report, too, which the Vicar Apostolic of Central Africa sent to the Superior of the Institute at Verona, Joshua received special and honourable mention.

Then the first World War broke out, one Father lost his life when the *Florence* was torpedoed in the Mediterranean, and several missionaries were interned. The upshot was that the Tonga mission had to be closed down, at least as a temporary measure, to the consternation of the natives who felt, and rightly felt, that in more senses than one, they were being left in the lurch. Joshua especially they were sorry to lose.

Patient and tactful, he had enough knowledge of their dialect to be able to make them laugh; and, when the parting came, there was a general outcry. "Yes, it is our own fault; he has been taken away because of our bad behaviour."

Transferred from Tonga to Lul, life for Joshua went on pretty much as before: the same climate and the same people, with the same moral and spiritual problems.

Opened in 1901, Lul was the first mission-station to be established among the Shilluk tribes. Its beginnings were marked by the usual difficulties and discouragements. For the first three years, the Register of Baptisms remained unopened. But, when the refugees from Tonga arrived in 1917, things were looking more promising. The conversions were going ahead, the original hovels had been replaced by decent premises, and a few Sisters were working alongside the priests and brothers. With all the building and excavating already done, it did seem as though Joshua could look forward to an easy life.

By this time, however, the superiors were well aware that he had other gifts and aptitudes. He was a practised hand at dealing with the natives and, while at Tonga, he had acquired a working knowledge of medicine from Brother Poloniato, who was known in the Sudan, and later in Uganda, as Hakim, the Doctor. It will be remembered that this Brother was the porter who had discovered Joshua on the doorstep eleven years before.

Joshua, therefore, exchanged the pick and shovel of the navvy for the bag and bedside manner of the professional doctor. No door was ever closed against him, and the patients, as usual, told him everything, including things he never knew before, things concerning the human anatomy which the Medical Faculty itself, had it been listening, must have heard for the first time. It was a strenuous business, with each day adding new patients to his panel. Eye trouble was one of the chief worries, with septic wounds and snake-bites recurring day by day. Fevers, of course, and even cases of leprosy. And always, the most obstinate thing to contend with, was the customary indifference of the victims, who were apt to pay no attention to their maladies until it was too late. Needless to say, there, as in our own part of the world, great numbers lined up at the clinic with nothing amiss that a dose of castor-oil, some quinine or a calomel pill could not cure, to say nothing of the traditional bottle of coloured water.

Meanwhile, the Doctor was neglecting himself and running risks that were to have serious consequences. His general health began to deteriorate and, in alarm, the Superior sent him to Khartum to recuperate.

"Here I am convalescing after a bout of malaria that has left me very tired. They say I need blood. The mosquitoes are to blame, for they have sucked it out of me."

The natives had their own way of dealing with this trouble. Before going to rest, they smeared their bodies with a layer of mud which they washed off first thing in the morning. The missionaries had, so far, not adopted this remedy, and Joshua went on to say that he had been going through a regular course of gymnastics, keeping the insects at bay.

7
HOMEWARD BOUND

THE midsummer of 1920 found the Valtellina in a state bordering on uproar. From the doors and balconies and across the narrow streets, the women were chattering at one another like magpies. Their menfolk, back from the war and now out in the fields and vineyards, were leaning on their forks and rakes, breaking or listening to the news.

"So, he is coming back, it seems."

"Che Cosa ? Who's coming ?"

"Why, Joshua Dei Cas. Poor Anacleto that we buried ! Well, it's his son. You remember."

"They say he is in Italy already."

"He's been out there for God knows how long, and they've let him come home."

"He's bound to show up here, I should think."

"In that case, we ought to do something about it. He didn't forget us, you know : I mean those letters of his . . ."

It was not only blood that Joshua needed but a complete change ; at least, so those in authority

---

Harbour on the Nile at Lull. The barge acts as a jetty for the boats which have scarcely changed since the time of the Pharaos.

began to think. Khartum was better than nothing, but its climate had anything but a good reputation. Presently, the order came from headquarters, and he turned about and headed for Cairo and for home. He had been thirteen years away.

So, the flags were up in the Valley; and when the missionary made his appearance, the houses and fields were abandoned and everybody who could walk turned out to meet him. The first comments were favourable enough. He was still the same man they had known; genial, jovial, and easy to approach and get on with. There was a regular bombardment of questions and answers. How many churches had he built? How many heathens had he baptised? Were the natives as savage as all that, and did they eat one another like so many Bologna sausages? What encounters had he had with the lions and the tigers?

Bearded and bronzed as his face was, his former work-mates thought he looked fine. But women's eyes are sharper, sharper by a long way.

"They may say what they like, but our Joshua is not well."

"Verissimo! You can see it: he's gone to nothing, he's as thin as a rake."

"O Poverino! Come é cambiato!"

"But is it any wonder? They tell me that out there it is nothing but sand; and unless you're a cannibal——"

"When he goes back, we must send him some of our sausages."

←

Slow but sure. A shilluk ship-building yard. One thing, they never make the mistake Robinson Crusoe made.

"And then the heat ! My neighbour says that they need no fires for cooking : the sun does it for you."

"Si, si : there is no doubt : his blood is dried up."

"Ah, if we could only send him some of our fresh air along with the sausages !"

"And Signora Matilda ! How sad she must be and her son so strong before. Do you remember . . .?"

Some of these details might not be admissable as evidence in a court-of-law ; but, on the whole, the women were not far wrong. Still, a good twelve months in Italy would be sure to put him on his feet.

He had returned to a sadly depleted household. Richard had been the first to go and his father had followed. Victor perished in an avalanche while serving with the Alpini in the war, and his mother survived for only twelve months. Naturally, the cemetery was the first thing to claim his attention and, there, he prayed for their souls and thanked God for all that they had meant, and still meant, to him. Too often, the departure of the mother means the break-up of the home, but somehow Teresina had managed to step into the breach and keep what was left together.

What a time of it they had, these two, the African correspondent and the sister who always got the first and the best of the news ! No need to tell her about his experiences over yonder. She had them all off by heart. She was able to make the most of the few weeks allowed. There was no cooking to be done, at any rate. The neighbours kept dropping in, day by day, bringing chickens and pigeons, home-made cakes and cheese, and bottles of their own first-rate wine.

While all this was going on, his future was being discussed by the superiors. Can we with any conscience, allow this lay-helper of ours to go on as he is to the end ? He had been neither clothed nor professed ; but as the Superior at Tonga put it : "We have taken the vows, but he has been beating us all at observing them, without having taken them at all." He might be clumsy enough, even now, and anything but 'the gentleman,' as we are pleased to call the man who cuts a fine dash ; but then some of the saints were never gentlemen, in that sense. Wouldn't it be right to let Joshua decide for himself ? It was a wise enough move and the response was soon forthcoming.

"My unworthiness apart, I know that the religious habit would not appear to advantage on my poor person. All the same, I would like to enter the novitiate and prepare for my Profession."

With his usual straightforwardness, he acknowledged that the comings and goings among the neighbours and the members of his family had thrown him a bit off his balance. "I hope, however, by God's grace, to return to my usual calm without much delay."

To make doubly sure, when the parting came, he warned them all that this time, and as far as this world was concerned, it was farewell for good.

With the expansion of their Institute, the Verona Fathers had opened a separate house for novices at Savona, where Pope Pius the Seventh spent some years in prison by courtesy of His Majesty Napoleon Bonaparte. Joshua arrived here on August 25th, fated, apparently, never to make a formal entry into a monastery otherwise than *incognito*. The door-keeper at Savona reports :

"He arrived at 8 o'clock in the evening carrying a heavy bag and wearing a light suit. I thought he was a railway-porter bringing along the luggage of one of our Fathers.

"What can I do for you ?"

"Is the Father Superior at home ?"

"Yes, do you want to give him that bag ?"

"No ; I would like to speak to him, if possible."

"Wait a second. I'll let him know."

Down came the Superior : embraces all round : collapse of the door-keeper.

The new novice was forty years old and already accustomed to the demands of a monastic life ; but, from first to last, he behaved with the docility of a postulant beginning from scratch. "He was an example and a spur to every one of us . . . His industry was a thing to wonder at : he invariably chose the hardest tasks . . . I can see him still, collected, tranquil, always in the best of humours and, on his return from the market, holding heart-to-heart conversations with a long-eared friend of his, the monastery donkey no less . . . Outsiders thought he was a simpleton, but only at first : they were never long in changing their minds."

These are some of the testimonies made later by those who had been in touch with him at this period ; but, alas, with that discriminating tendency common to all historians, they have omitted to hand down the name of the donkey to posterity.

Brother Joshua had been entrusted with the monastic purse, which meant a daily visit to the market, in the company of the long-eared friend aforesaid. Much too shrewd by nature, and made more so by his responsibility, Joshua was not the one to be imposed on by the glib tongues of the stall-holders. Some deal or other with a fishmonger, who turned out to be an Arab, led to a mild altercation, during which the woman tried to do a bit of cursing in her own tongue. Joshua kept

84

his temper, and replied with a few forthright words in the same language. The woman ended up as a Christian and a consistent benefactor of the Missions.

The novices hailed from many separate localities, mostly in the north ; and, as part of their training, they had to have a course of instruction in their own language. Manzoni has told us how, before writing the book which even now ranks as a literary classic, he went down to Florence, where the best Italian is spoken, in order to rinse out his mouth with the waters of the Arno. Since these novices were familiar only with their own dialects, it was thought well to subject them to the same treatment. They had to read and study the best authors, and they had to write compositions of their own. It must have surprised them to find that Joshua required hardly any tuition at all. For years, he had been reading respectable authors, if not the best ones, in the shape of articles in the Press, the writers of which, at that time, maintained a fairly high level of culture. At any rate, his essays usually managed to earn full marks.

In the meantime, his sister Teresina was on the look-out for the postman. She hadn't long to wait.

"There are forty-six of us novices here, some of them what you might call boys except, perhaps, your humble servant. There are a few clerics, as well, studying theology, philosophy, gastronomy, astronomy and I don't know what. Ex-soldiers for the most part, there are two at least who, not so long ago, were firing bullets at one another, because one of them is from the Trentino and had to fight for the Kaiser."

What with his experiences, unusual in a novice, and the flair he had for joking and telling good stories, he was in great demand at recreation.

"Brother Joshua, you've been among the Negroes long enough. Show us how they do their dances."

Joshua looked round for something that might serve as a lance and, with a curtain pole or something in his hand, he went through his paces, red in the face with confusion but egged on by the applause of the spectators.

At the end of sixteen months he was ready to be professed. As a preliminary, he had to make some sort of a will by way of divesting himself of his private property. Nothing could be more business-like than the letter he wrote on this subject to his two brothers.

"Listen ! Our rule obliges us to make a will before taking the vows. Well, knowing how badly off you are, I herewith renounce, in your favour, the share I could claim in the family inheritance. In the event of either or both of you becoming Franciscans, say, then my share must not be given to St. Francis, but must be returned to the African Missions. If that never happens, and you find yourselves in fairly comfortable circumstances, I rely on you not to forget our Missions, whose needs you can read all about in our magazine *Nigrizia*. Just write back at once and say if you agree. This is an unusual style of letter to come from me, but don't imagine that I've suddenly gone all glum and gloomy. Not a bit of it. Glum and gloom is only for those with plenty of cash in their pockets. Fortunately for us, ours are always empty."

The Profession, which took place at midnight on Christmas Eve, meant that he was now at last a fully-fledged Son of the Sacred Heart entitled to wear the habit and the cross of the Congregation. Everyone was delighted except the chickens.

86

"On Christmas morning, I prepared the mash and went down to the hen-run. Instead of the usual hub-bub, with the poultry charging at me and leaping on to the bucket, they all turned tail and made off. They just didn't know me in the habit. Even when they had settled down, they kept looking up from the feed as though they still had their doubts."

A week later he left for Verona *en route* for Africa, and the same day the Master of Novices, in open conference, told those who were left that they had parted from the humblest member of the whole Order.

He was at liberty to run up to the Valley again for a final farewell, but he wouldn't risk it. As he said, the tears he had shed into his beard the last time had now dried out, and there was no sense in making them flow all over again. So he wrote instead.

"On the point of leaving Italy for the second time, my message to you all is *Salaam Aleicum*, which in Arabic means Peace be to you. Don't quarrel among yourselves whatever you do. There is nothing for it but to forgive those who have done us an injury. Have you never heard of a thing called Death ? And how will you feel if God, for a joke, were to make a next-door neighbour of the one you are so angry with ? I remember how, when I was living at home, poor Marinin and old Joseph had a falling-out. Well, they went off to the Mayor and had a regular tug-of-war in his presence. At last, they agreed to have some Masses said, and off they went quite contented with one another. There is no reason why that experiment should not be tried again.

"The other day, the Superior said to me : 'That sister of yours seems to be a wise woman. Tell her to send some of her wisdom along to us.' Well, Teresina, don't let what I'm telling you turn your head : I myself am in no danger on that score ; and, having less wisdom means that the account we shall all have to render will not be so strict in my case . . . You tell me that our Superiors have made you a promoter of our magazine *Nigrizia*. Congratulations! I am not envious. Try to carry on the work after I am gone. You ask me am I well : I wish the bread I eat every morning could answer that question for me. What am I studying ? I am studying how to dig a place for myself in the corner of paradise and, in my spare time, I dig in the garden and do some planting. Am I happy ? I could jump for joy, and is it any wonder. Here I am getting ready to go to Africa to help those poor people who know nothing of the One who shed his blood for them. If you have any more Joshuas up there, send them along and we shall turn them into missionaries. And it would be a fine thing if the good folk in Piatta could scrape together a few pence to help these seminarists of ours, who have sacrificed their youth and their liberty, in order to carry the light of faith to the descendants of Cain. Those who have to feed and clothe them are sometimes hard put to make ends meet."

The little party arrived in Rome in time for the funeral of Pope Benedict the Fifteenth and left Naples a week later, arriving in Cairo in due course. On Good Friday, they were once again in the mission-station at Lul, where Joshua resumed his former occupations : market-gardener, mason, family doctor and general factotum. "I am sending you a useless Brother"—this was the message St. Gerard carried from one superior to another, when he was more or less forcing his way into the Redemptorist Order. No one in his senses could, at any time, have lodged that complaint against the latest addition to Bishop Comboni's Institute. And now he was back in the trenches, so to say, and ready for the fray. The day was fast approaching when he was to become a casualty, and be carried for good to the rear. But, while even a remnant of his former health and strength remained, he would stick to his post in the front line, constantly under fire from the insect bites and the remorseless equatorial sun.

———

8
NO BIGGER THAN A MAN'S HAND

THINGS in Africa were going ahead at such a rate that, before the end of twelve months, Joshua was chosen, along with three others, to tackle the difficult business of starting a new mission-station. This was to be at a place called Detwok, which lies on the bank of the White Nile north of Lul ; a tolerable enough settlement as such settlements go, a sandy soil protected from the heat by a species of olive trees and by thorn bushes. There were, of course, the usual marshes, with malaria in close attendance ; but there were plenty of villages with some forty thousand inhabitants, all belonging to the Shilluk tribe.

As a necessary preliminary, one of the Fathers was sent on ahead to come to terms with King Ayoke, who ruled over the district from his palace in Fashoda, and then with the representative of the British government. His Majesty consented readily, because he was on friendly terms with the missionaries and knew the good work they were doing for his people. The next thing was to go and spy out the promised land. To make the journey easier, the King ordered the state donkey to be fed and saddled, and placed at Father Kohnen's disposal—in the eyes of the natives, a royal gesture and no mistake.

The site having been chosen and the government informed, an English officer arrived by boat to see for himself what was proposed.

"Is this what you're thinking about, Father ? Can't you find anything better ?"

"Not exactly a charming spot, I agree : but for our purposes it is just the thing."

"Oh, very good. There's one worry you needn't be afraid of, no one is likely to want to take it from you."

The party, complete with bag and baggage, sailed from Lul in the *Scibaloka*, a boat placed at their disposal by the British governor. We can take it that Joshua was not the last to jump ashore. He would be among the Shilluk again, and it would be all pioneering work, building and draining and planting, the sort of thing he enjoyed more than anything. Within six months he was down with a bad attack of malaria and was sent back to Lul to recover. Being on his own, he spent most of the time on board with the stokers down in the engine-room.

On the way to the new foundation at Detwok, one of the Fathers noticed that the fingers of one of his hands looked somewhat raw and lacerated. He paid no great attention to it, however, because this was nothing very new in one whose hands were hardly ever free from the marks of the rough usage they were used to getting. But the thing became so noticeable that, at last, he questioned him about it.

"That hand of yours, what's the matter with it ? And the other one ; it's very nearly as bad. What have you been doing ?"

"Oh, it's nothing. I scalded myself a bit, if you want to know."

"Come now, that won't do. They look really sore to me. Are they sore ?"

"Not at all. That's the best of it or the worst of it. To tell the truth, that's what's bothering me. I can hold them in the fire without feeling anything."

An alarming revelation !

By this time, the African missionaries knew that these symptoms pointed, not necessarily but almost certainly, in one direction. Having satisfied himself that the affected fingers were quite insensitive to the prick of a needle, the Father wrote to Khartum to get the opinion of the Syrian doctor who was in practice there. He thought it might be diabetes and prescribed accordingly. There was relief all round, and Joshua went on with his work determined to put the thing out of his mind.

This anxiety was hardly over, when news came from Detwok that the founder of the new station, and its first superior, had been carried off by cerebrospinal meningitis, one of the scourges of Central Africa at that time, which was taking its toll of the missionaries, usually with a marked partiality for the younger ones. Black Fever, as it is called, is sudden in its onset, and may do its deadly work in a matter of weeks or even days. The stages of the malady are painful and distressing in the extreme. Father Beduschi was an old friend of Joshua's. They had gone to Tonga together and then to Detwok, and now he was dead after four short months in office. "He was a hard worker," Joshua wrote to Teresina. "He hardly ever rested. A good part of the night he spent in writing, and the little sleep he got was taken on the stairs or in the church."

Shortly after pronouncing his final vows in the temporary chapel made of mud and straw, Joshua was taken ill again, and had to sail to Khartum with one of the priests and a couple of Sisters. The Duchess of Aosta, who was touring Africa at the time, was on the quay when the boat landed and spoke a few words to the new arrivals. Then she drew the priest aside.

"Are you aware that there is something seriously wrong with that Brother of yours ? You ought to see to it without delay."

"Yes, I'm afraid it is only too true. We are on our way to have it looked into."

The skin-specialist was a hard man, hardened no doubt by his own hard experiences, and with scant respect for the feelings of his patients. One look at Joshua was enough.

"Why, this is leprosy and in an advanced stage, too. Get outside, will you, before you infect my surgery !"

Leprosy, of course, is not infectious at all, not in that way. Casual contacts with the complaint can do no harm. But that was not understood in those days, when the ancient terror was still abroad in the land. We might stretch a point in favour of the doctor's callousness, which might have been just the chilly impersonal detachment of the professional man. As for the victim himself, when he got back to the community, he re-enacted the scene, laughing heartily the while as though it were more a joke than anything else. We may be sure that this display of high spirits was only a cover-up for his real feelings. He had seen for himself what leprosy can do to a human being, the devastating inroads it makes into one's physical appearance, it's psychological effects, probably more devastating still. But the verdict of the specialist was no bolt from the blue. That was something. He had been getting used to the idea for four years, quietly strengthening his spiritual defences and looking the facts in the face.

"My hands," he writes home, "have been going numb for quite a while, and the doctor was worried about my bones which, I assure you, are quite intact and still in their places. He thought the thing might be——; well, never mind ; although I must confess that, for the moment, I felt as though I were facing a firing-squad. Let's see how all this will end, bearing in mind that I can't possibly be indispensable to the Missions, since, after fifteen years, I haven't been able to convert myself. *Fiat voluntas tua.*"

One suggestion is that our illnesses are sent to us as a corrective, that they are meant to take us down a peg, and thus restore the balance of our minds so easily overset by the prevailing *superbia vitae*. But while our ailments can be humiliating enough, some more than others, leprosy for thousands of years was reckoned a personal disgrace, like crucifixion, which Cicero tells us was of all punishments the most cruel and the most feared. Leprosy was a divine judgment or, failing that, something preternatural, an emanation from the underworld. In primitive lands this is largely the view taken of it at the present day.

> One struck by God and afflicted. He shall be reckoned among the unclean and shall have his clothes loose, his head bare, his mouth covered with a cloth, and he shall cry out that he is defiled and shall dwell alone without the camp.

It is now known that this is an ordinary, natural complaint, a bacterial disease resembling tuberculosis. The experts consider that the ultimate conquest of the malady is a certainty. If medical services could be so expanded as to reach all the infected areas, it might disappear in a quarter of a century ; thanks to the group of drugs called Sulphones, a recent discovery, which can guarantee a cure at the end of a two years' treatment. It is an expensive medicine and the whole course costs about twelve guineas.

But the disease is still a mystery to some extent. Apparently, it is not yet known how it is transmitted from one person to another, nor yet why whole areas of the globe are infected, leaving adjoining areas unmolested. For example, it is rife in Brazil and almost unheard of in Chile. In certain parts of Africa, as much as ten per cent. of the population is affected. Although it progresses by slow stages, the average expectation of life for a leper is ten years.

With ordinary everyday precautions, no missionary need ever have to carry this extra burden of affliction. Those who have had to do so were mostly pioneers of several Christian denominations, whose lot it was, as pioneers, to make all the mistakes, in order that those who followed on might not make them.

Had Joshua Dei Cas been other than he was, he might have escaped to die of old age. Being himself, eager, impetuous, self-effacing, and heedless of risks where the risks interposed between his safety and the claims of charity, it was discovered, when it was too late, that at Tonga he had literally been rubbing shoulders with a leper, a poor old man living apart, neglected and shunned, without nose, lips, hands and feet. Every chance he got, he was off into the jungle, bringing food and any likely medicine that he got hold of. Then there was a certain Stephen Ayong, one of

The little Chapel in the leper colony where Brother Joshua spent all his spare time and where Mass was said regularly. "My Cathedral", he called it.

96

the richest and most influential men in the district, who contracted the disease and began to frequent the mission-station. Joshua nursed and clothed him, fed him and let him eat out of his own plate : proceedings which, if known, must have shaken Harley Street to its foundations.

Pascal thought that nothing is so insupportable to man as having to keep still and "sit quietly in one's room without business, without passion, without study, without diversion. So hastes our life away." Once the truth was known, perhaps the hardest battle Joshua had to fight was against his own energetic urges, the will to be up and doing, the activity-habit he had acquired in his native mountains, and had developed later in the mission-stations. A person of this build comes to have such faith in the stability of his own body, that the possibility of his being incapacitated, as others are, seems so remote as to be practically non-existent. Nothing disturbs this confidence for very long at a time ; and, even when we have a suspicion that the unseen enemy is watching and waiting to spring upon its prey, we still cherish the idea that we may be able to shake him off. When at last we are forced to knuckle under, our inability to break out of the prison seems to be a monstrous thing, as unthinkable as being compelled to remain shut up in a house that is on fire. As one confirmed invalid puts it :

"In face of this cruel persistence and the failure of all the remedies that were tried, I at last understood, what every fibre of my being rebelled against, that the

←
Brother Joshua (left centre back row) with some of his fellow lepers young and old. Note the Cross surmounting the hut. 'Per Crucem ad Lucem'.

malady would never slacken its grip, any more than a vulture will relinquish what it holds in its beak and claws."

Brother Joshua experienced little or none of this extreme perturbation or near-panic. His letters make it clear that he had never looked forward to an easy or a long life, had never tried to persuade himself that the visitations to which we frail mortals are subjected would pass him by. The will of God under all circumstances—his mind had been quite made up on that and from the very start. For all these reasons, the onset of his malady did not take him off his guard. He was under no sudden necessity of readjusting his ideas, a difficult task when it has to be entered on amid the confusion of mind entailed by the actual illness. His spiritual weapons had been forged long since, and he had kept them sharp and free from rust. Self-pity he never seems to have had any time for and, up to the end, he was spared that aggravating complication.

Was he not a Christian and, therefore, drawn within the circle of Christ's redeeming activity ; the activity of Him Who has not chosen to do His work in isolation from His members, and Who made it plain that they are called upon to make up, by their own contribution, for what is wanting to His own passion and death ; to tip the scales, so to say ?

And, after all, he was not the only one. There was Father Beduschi himself, the Superior at Detwok. Just when everything was beginning to look so promising, he was struck down and died offering his life for the people he was working for. When he was at the point of death his companion, Father Brambilla, tried to buy a bottle of milk, from these same people, as a comfort for the dying man. But they refused: their ingrained hostility was too much for them.

Sister Christina, who was in close contact with Joshua all through the crisis of his illness, testified that he never gave one the impression that he thought himself badly used. "He spoke of his illness with extraordinary frankness, and would often hold his fingers up, and remark that soon they would be out of the way and would give no more trouble. He was firmly convinced, too, that his missionary apostolate was only really beginning, since he could offer up his sufferings for the souls of the natives: "And all this," she concludes, "could only be the result of a consistent and well-developed spiritual outlook."

———————

9
THE DARKENING CLOUD

FROM now on, the small cloud that had so suddenly appeared on the horizon was to grow larger and more menacing.

Gesira is a healthy island formed by the Nile and the *Bahr-el-Ama,* and situated about an hour's walk from Cairo. In 1888, the Verona Fathers had bought an extensive plot on this island, and had established there a kind of refugee camp for those Negroes who had escaped from or been released by their slave-masters, or had fled from the interior of the country in order to avoid being carried off to the markets. After the Mahdist rising, which was crushed at Omdurman by Lord Kitchener's troops, the colony had been abandoned. Some of the inmates died, others had returned to their villages, others again had got work in the city. The house was, therefore, turned into a rest-centre for the sick or exhausted members of the Institute.

Joshua arrived here in the summer of 1925 and remained for three years. He was given a small room on the ground floor, and a reserved seat in the refectory and chapel.

He was never a danger to the community. Able to be about and on his feet, he needed hardly any attention. The dishes he used at table and the bandages covering his fingers he washed for himself. He showed great agility and artfulness in keeping out of the way; and, when anyone approached, he would draw himself up like a sentry and cry out: "Halt! Stop where you are, please!" When visitors called at the hostel, he would make himself scarce lest the sight of his face and hands might stop them from coming to church. The Sisters belonging to the community were accommodated in a separate building and, as often as he had occasion to go there, he used a stick for opening the gate and ringing the bell. Always the first to arrive in the chapel, he knelt on the last bench close against the wall, and took care not to lean on the altar-rails when receiving Holy Communion.

He was allowed to potter about and do odds and ends of small jobs, but he was under obedience to leave anything involving effort severely alone. This inactivity was one of his biggest trials and, in a letter to the Superior General, he made no secret of the fact.

"You ask me if I am doing what I am told. Well, the the only order I've received so far is to do nothing, and that's a job that doesn't suit me."

Once the temptation was too strong for him. While workmen were repairing the church, Joshua would sometimes sit in his place at the back and watch them. One day he noticed that something or other up near the roof needed putting to rights. No one was about and, before you could say knife, he was up the ladder to see what could be done. He was caught red-handed. One of the Fathers came in, at the same moment, and he was told to come down out of that.

No! It was no joke getting used to this enforced idleness. From the days when he toiled amongst the natives, work, and hard work, had been an integral part of his spiritual life, a thing consecrated to the service of Him Who was reputed to be the Son of a Carpenter. It was not only that, for him, every common bush was afire with God, but he found the grace and joy of the Holy Spirit emanating from the heaviest tasks and the meanest employments.

The slow-passing hours and days were not empty for all that. As the *Osservatore Romano* kept coming to hand, he would sit on a stone in the grounds and read it from cover to cover. He had any number of friends, besides, those who were not afraid to approach him for their own sake as well as for his. He would listen to their troubles and difficulties and give them advice. The Apostolic Delegate to Egypt, Bishop Valerio Valeri, in particular, never failed to send him greetings and inquire after his health.

But it was the poorest of the poor who came oftenest, the *meskins*, who felt that he was a *meskin* like themselves and would be sure to understand. He could speak Arabic fairly well and was studying all the time, jotting down in a note-book each new word as it cropped up.

"Sometimes when he went out," one of the Sisters tells us, "the street-arabs, seeing the state he was in, thought he was the worse for drink. Then they would start booing and throwing stones at him. But Joshua just joined in the booing and, picking up the stones, started to juggle with them."

He did quite a good business on the side, in patching up those squabbles between married couples that seem to be confined to no part of the habitable globe. And he was very artful, indeed, in the way he went to work with them ; for he would take the husband aside and convince him that his wife was one of the best women in the world, and after that it would be the wife's turn.

The medical clinic he attended regularly, always taking his place at the end of the queue and at some distance apart.

Up in the Valtellina, nobody knew what to think. "There's something the matter with Joshua, but he doesn't tell us a thing." And so they sent off a peremptory letter.

"You ask me what disease I have got. I can only tell you it's a disease not to be found in Piatta and, had I remained there, I wouldn't have caught it myself. It's just that my hands are numb, which means that nothing you do to them can make them hurt. They tell me that I shall die of it. But that is nothing unusual. We must all die of something, sooner or later ; and, if it is sooner for me, what's the odds ! It's God's will, isn't it ? As for you, Louis, if, as you say, you have appendicitis, for goodness sake see to it. If you don't have an operation, you'll be stealing a march on me and getting there first. Very nice to be sure ; but, at the moment, the operation is your immediate duty."

There was an old friend of his still living in Italy, one of the engineers with whom he had worked in the Pass, and to him alone he disclosed his secret. This friend had given up the practice of his religion long before, and now he was laid up with tuberculosis. Joshua wrote to him regularly in an effort to get him back to his duties, and now he made a last bid for it.

"You are in hospital, I see, and with consumption. But let me tell you, my case is harder to bear than yours. I've got leprosy, in fact, and believe it or not, I am happy, because the Lord has given me this chance of making some kind of preparation for death."

"If only I could get back to the mission-station in the Sudan among my negroes"—that was the thought haunting him night and day. The superiors had made several attempts to find a suitable hospital in which he could receive the medical attention he now required. There was a leper-colony on the island of Cyprus which offered a fair chance of a cure, but there were no religious facilities available in it, and it was felt that such a hardship added to the isolation of the place would do Joshua more harm than good. They submitted his case to the governors of the Mauritian Hospital in Turin and they agreed to accept him. But, in the face of the sanitary laws then in vogue, no ship dared undertake to convey him across the Mediterranean.

Then, one day, a missionary from the *Bahr-el-Ghazal* province, the one-time home of the Shilluk tribe, stopped at Gesira ; and Joshua and he were soon comparing notes regarding the work going on there.

"Brother, have you heard that the British Government has opened a leper-colony at Khor-Melang ?"

"At Khor-Melang ! Are you sure of that ?"

"Positive. Some of the huts are up already and there will soon be plenty more, because all the lepers in the neighbourhood are going to be rounded-up and put into them, whether they like it or not. We are going to look after the religious side of the project. It's a good idea."

It was a good idea and, after thinking about it for some time, one good idea followed another. "Why shouldn't I go to the colony—as a patient ? I could be a patient and a missionary at the same time, and it would put an end to the worry the Superiors are having about me. I can't stop here much longer ; that's plain enough. It's not safe. Khor-Melang would be the right thing in the right place, because it's between Detwok and Tonga, in the very thick of my old comrades the Shilluk."

When it was first put to them, the Superiors shook their heads ; and no wonder, for the accommodation and conveniences provided by the new colony were, so far, of the most primitive kind—huts of mud and straw, erected in a spot miles away from the nearest villages ; and, what's more, it was exclusively for Negroes, many of whom were in the last stages of the malady. How could you allow a member of a Religious Order to end his days in such surroundings, and such days as his had been ? It just wouldn't do.

By degrees, however, objections to the proposal began to grow less and less. The man chiefly concerned was so keen on the thing, that the merest sign from the authorities would have sent him scampering off that very day. Then, with him on the spot and with the same cross to bear, the poor wretches would have the next best thing to a real chaplain, one whose example and adroit way of talking could not but be a tremendous help to them. Joshua might be impetuous, rather too insistent on having his own way, but his way might well be God's way. That climbing of his over the wall at Verona, that was impetuosity, if you like. But looking back now at all that had happened since, it was evident that the finger of God had played a big part in it.

The Vicar Apostolic of the district in which the leper-colony was situated was Monsignor Anthony

Stoppani, nephew of the geologist Abbot Stoppani. As soon as he heard of the proposal, he wrote to say that nothing was better calculated to bring a blessing upon the new scheme than the presence among the lepers of a Brother of such spiritual calibre, whose virtues and very sufferings would be to the advantage of everybody concerned.

The government officials could hardly be expected to see things quite in the same light. There was a lot of haggling with, we may suppose, the usual question-naires to be filled up, in triplicate of course. But at last, the passport was stamped and signed, and nothing remained but to provide the Brother with a dwelling a little in keeping with his status as a missionary. The money was soon collected, and every member of the local religious community rolled up his sleeves, and went to work to build a house with a small chapel attached in which Mass would be said as often as possible. It stood on a hillock overlooking the river Giur, a twenty minutes cycle ride from Wau, the mission-station, and about a mile from the colony proper.

This colony was not a hospital in any sense of the word, any more than Molokai was, even in its best days. It was more of a concentration camp than any-thing, a widely-scattered village in which the victims lived in separate huts, alongside those who might be from different tribes speaking different languages. In this compound, the natives, deprived of their freedom, tended their crops and did some manual work when possible ; and, for the rest, waited for death to come and set them free. An even worse fate must have been theirs had they remained at home ; for there, there was no pity for them any more than for the lepers of old. Out they had to go into the wilderness where they usually died of hunger or sheer neglect. As it was, there was enough to eat, plenty of medicine and the fairly regular services of religion.

Short of having actually seen one, it is not easy for us to form a proper idea of what Lazarettoes were like at the time of their first formation. To the consideration of the subject, we bring something of the terror which the mere mention of the word leper inspired during thousands of years. Job called the disease "the first-born of death" and the Egyptians, in their turn, could think of no better name for it than "death before death"; apt enough descriptions, since decomposition and the *rigor mortis* can supervene while the victim is still alive.

Robert Louis Stevenson had seen for himself; and, although he was writing under what he believed to be an impelling provocation and, therefore, may have unconsciously overdrawn the picture, the picture is grim enough even with every allowance made.

". . . the abominable deformations of our common manhood, a population as only now and then surrounds us in the horror of a nightmare . . . every fourth face a blot on the landscape . . . butt-ends of human beings lying there almost unrecognisable, but still breathing, still thinking, still remembering . . . It is not the fear of possible infection : that seems a little thing when compared with the pain, the pity, the disgust of the visitor's surroundings, and the atmosphere of affliction and physical disgrace which he breathes."

This was Molokai, where Father Damien lived and worked and suffered, for most of the time unaided and alone. At no time was Khor-Melang as bad as that. English doctors were in attendance. There was a

Christian catechist among the patients, and he took charge of a class for prospective converts, and the Nuns from Wau visited the colony as a matter of routine and went the round of the huts, distributing gifts of nuts and dates.

Then, on top of all, Joshua arrived and Khor-Melang had a missionary of its own, a leper still fairly active except for his hands, and as keen as mustard to begin. "Who could be happier than I" was his first reaction, and then he settled down to write to the Superior General in Italy, begging him not to let any of his relations know. A month later, he penned another diplomatic letter to his brothers.

"I am still alive as you see, and am now here at Wau, where our founder, Bishop Comboni, stayed forty years ago. As far as work is concerned, I do little or nothing except light jobs, such as looking after the cows. Although the irritation in my hands has not improved, I live like a lord."

But the news leaked out all the same. On opening the March number of the magazine *Nigrizia* there it was in black and white, and a weekly newspaper published in Como devoted an article to it under the heading :

A Missionary From Our Diocese Struck
With Leprosy.

His sister, Teresina, sent off an urgent demand for an explanation and for a true account of the state of his health.

Joshua replied: "So, you've been reading *Nigrizia* have you ! And you seem to be unhappy and are blaming me for my secrecy. But dear me ! What have I been doing for the past four or five years except sending you bulletins about my health. I am not dead and isn't that good enough for you ? Don't swallow everything you read in newspapers. I am not in pain and I am not in bed : and yet you seem to imagine that the world is coming to an end. Don't worry, I tell you. I feel well, and I am the only one in our Society who can truthfully say that he doesn't have to give a thought to tomorrow."

10
A LEPER AMONG LEPERS

KHOR-MELANG was described as a Black Hell, *Inferno Nero;* a pardonable overstatement constantly recurring in our everyday language, and a tribute, mostly an unconscious tribute, paid to the realities of that most formidable of all religious mysteries.

Lasciate ogni speranza, voi ch'entrate.

At any rate, none of the hells we are acquainted with need display that grim message over its portals ; and, whatever may have been the position at Khor-Melang in the first instance, with the arrival of Brother Joshua, hope and hope at its very best sprang up in the hearts of the inmates.

The small villa built for him by his brethren soon became the moral and spiritual centre round which the colony revolved. His door was never closed ; and, in ones and twos and threes, these stricken people came to him with their grievances and their sorrows, and none ever left without carrying away some grains of consolation and of comfort. It was not long before

→

All things to all men. Group showing brother Joshua with Brother Gatti on his left and Brother Zanetti on his right. The ravages of the disease can be seen on the lepers.

he was calling himself "the feudatory of Khor-Melang," the Big Chief or Lord of the Manor, whose subjects had learnt to know the kind of person he was, and flocked to his audience-chamber. Reports reached the distant villages that there was a funny man living "over there" who could do tricks, and was always laughing. Presently the children, like children everywhere, had found a way of getting at him and were invading the veranda of his home at all hours.

Although some of the languages spoken by the patients were quite unfamiliar, he worked hard to master the rudiments of these dialects, and to translate the prayers and the leading questions of the catechism. In two months, he was able to say the Our Father, the Hail Mary and other prayers in the Ndogo language. He regarded the lepers as his parishioners, and himself as their parish priest in everything except the grace of ordination ; and, very soon, the business of catechizing was in full swing.

"In December I baptized my first convert, an old woman with a broken arm. I christened her Matilda after my own mother. Next, I had two more, one a leper with the death-rattle already in his throat, and the other a woman whom I named Teresina. Her hands had already disappeared and she was carrying a baby, a mere skeleton. It was just plain starvation, and we were able to put the life back into it again."

On the morning of September 15th, 1929, there was a ceremony in the church when eleven natives were publicly baptized, eight of them lepers. They had

←

Brother Joshua's sister Teresina, present day, still living with the youngest brother Riccardo and the old farm, active and smiling while looking forward to the eternal re-union.

been attending the classes for two years, some of them crawling on all fours and others having to be wheeled in a barrow. One old man had been a professional entertainer in his time, going from village to village playing the ronde and singing serenades. Then leprosy struck at his family. His wife died of it, and he himself went blind and lost the use of his legs. An unusually intelligent man, with a good memory carried over from his experiences on the stage, he became an enthusiastic catechumen. After the solemn Mass, there was feasting all round, sugar-canes and dates by the plateful, and a distribution of salt and tobacco. The tobacco was usually smoked in a big pipe passed from one man to another.

Before the Mass was due to begin on Sundays, the native catechist went from hut to hut with a cart drawn by two oxen, in order to collect the worst cases. This was a great event for the children, who scrambled up behind and sat on the shafts, while the less fortunate ran alongside until they reached the chapel. And then it was a sight for sore eyes to see the way Joshua welcomed them at the door, handing them out one by one as though they were grandees. *Cortesia* was one of St. Francis' Fair Ladies, and both the word and the gracious thing for which the word stands are products of Italy. And, although this lay brother might be conspicuous for a certain floundering awkwardness, all are agreed that these external traits of character never interfered with his good manners.

Each night was set apart for visits to the huts and he tells how, once when going his rounds, an old woman came out and asked him to walk across her little plot of land, because, as she said, "the earth is always better when you have passed over it."

One of his constant anxieties was the shortage of food, since the distribution made by the government was often quite inadequate ; a little meat now and then and, once a week, a portion of wheat which the lepers had to grind for themselves.

"One morning," says the visiting Infirmarian, Brother Gatti, "I arrived at the huts a little earlier than usual, only to find Joshua disposing of the parcel of eatables we had sent along for his own use. When I remonstrated with him, he told me that there was no danger of his ever starving because, with having nothing to do, he was growing much too fat. 'In any case,' he added, 'I have the Superior's permission for what I am doing'."

He treated the parcels he received from Italy in the same way.

"Dear Brother. Everything you have sent is most useful, specially that salame and those sweets, a good share of which will go into the black mouths that are waiting for them. And, if you can, send some fish-hooks or the money to buy them."

Fish-hooks and more fish-hooks : that was the cry. What with the food-shortage and the need to keep his fellow-lepers occupied, Joshua had started a Fishing Club which everybody joined, everybody who could get as far as the river, whether on their feet, on all-fours, in wheel-barrows or on the backs of their companions. And thanks to their chaplain, fish-hooks were soon coming over from Italy in their thousands, at a cost of twenty-five lire for five hundred.

Expert at handling either the harpoon or the net, the Shilluk are fishermen bred to the art from their earliest youth. During the three months of the year, when the river level is at its lowest, the whole village turns out, women and all, carrying cooking pots as well as the necessary tackle. What the spears fail to do, the nets make up for; and, in the early evening, everyone returns home tired and laden with the spoil. While these expeditions are on, the schools have to be given a day off, as a matter of course, and if the catch has been a good one, the pupils do not turn up until all the fish has been eaten.

The announcement in the Como newspaper that a native of the district had gone down with leprosy, turned a great number of hearts in the direction of Central Africa, and brought useful supplies to the colony, besides inquiries from responsible bodies as to the requirements of the Mission. With his usual common sense, Joshua went into the practical details.

To Professor Monachesi of Bormio he wrote as follows:

"You ask what gifts you ought to send. As you know, most of my parishioners are lepers and, when they come to Mass, we like to see them well dressed for the occasion. So send shirts and trousers, if you can afford it. You'll see: interest and capital will be returned to you by the Lord. Everything is useful here, from church-vestments to clothing for the inmates. And money, if you like, which will buy needles and thread, string, flour, salt, safety-matches and, of course, fish-hooks. Every day one or other comes along to me with the same request: Brother, will you give me a fish-hook?

"That salame of yours has arrived safe and sound. Fortunately, in the corner of the newspaper you sent with it, you had written 'From your cousin Henry,' otherwise I should never have known who the sender was. In my time, there was a lad called Martin Praulin, who used to climb up into the belfry of our church, so that no one might see him devouring his salame. I shall eat yours at the table, for you must know that I have such an article of furniture here, not like when I was at home and had to eat my lunch sitting on a box. Keep on sending a sausage now and again, after I am gone. Somebody else will have the benefit of them."

In 1931 there was a notable plague of locusts which Joshua, in one of his letters, describes at some length, for the benefit of those happily unacquainted with this sinister phenomenon of nature. He was not to know, any more than his relations, that a swarm had actually reached Lombardy in the late Middle Ages. For that matter, a swarm actually reached England in 1869.

"They came," he says, "in their millions, wave after wave, and then fell from the sky like snow in winter." This report certainly tallies with the accounts to be found in the text-books, which speak of them as darkening the sun like a blanket and then, like a blanket, descending to the earth. Apparently, the Arabic name for the locusts is derived from this feature of their behaviour : they are the "light-extinguishers." Nothing can daunt this living and moving blanket, neither injury nor death. Having devoured everything, the swarm will move off as a swarm, as though impelled by some sort of electronic power. If a river lies in the way, the top layer will settle on the water, heedless of the risk, and act like a bridge over which the rest follow like a vast army on the move, in perfect step and formation.

It is not surprising that this plague, which after all,

was one of those visited on Egypt at the divine command, has been and still is regarded with superstitious horror as being, like leprosy, something appertaining to the domain of the enemy of mankind. Some of the early Christian heretics brought the locusts forward as a tangible proof that there were two Gods, a bad one as well as a good one; while one Arabian writer described them as having "the head of a horse, the eyes of an elephant, the neck of a bull, the horns of a stag, the breast of a lion, the belly of a scorpion, the wings of an eagle, the legs of a camel, the feet of an ostrich, and the tail of a serpent."

It was the mystery of the thing that excited the imagination of the ancients. Their foraging expeditions are haphazard and irregular without known rhyme or reason. And it is not only what they devour. Having exterminated every living plant, they proceed to corrupt the barren soil with a slimy exudation, and end up by dying on the spot and tainting the very air with their decomposing corpses.

In his letter, Joshua tells how his villagers stole a march on the animals before they had time to do their worst by dying.

"Some of our lepers are used to eating locusts and, at night, they went out and filled whole sacks. They are quite good, too, they tell me. And I can well believe it, since John the Baptist practically lived on them while he was in the wilderness."

Unfortunately, the Higher Critics are not disposed to accept this last item of information. What John the Baptist favoured was the locust bean, "rich in carbohydrates and albumenoids" which, when ground, makes excellent sugar. Sixty and seventy years ago, in Scotland, we children bought and ate these beans as a regular thing.

None of all his plodding for others was allowed to interfere with his own spiritual life. That was the activating principle behind everything, the power-house whence he drew his daily and much-needed allowance of courage, energy and cheerfulness. To neglect that would be like sawing off the very branch that was supporting him, the branch drawing the sap of life from the parent vine which is no other than Christ himself. He never omitted the religious exercises prescribed by the rule of his Order and, in order not to lose the extra grace promised to those who come together for common prayer, he did his level best to keep to the appointed hours laid down in the time-table.

For the rosary, he gathered round him a make-shift community consisting of the neighbours and the servant who looked after his house, five or six altogether. Up at cock-crow, in the freshness of the early morning, with the impressive stillness of the landscape about him, he made his hour's meditation, and got ready for the Mass at which he received Holy Communion.

"Let him who thinks to stand take heed lest he fall." With that warning in mind, he neglected none of the traditional precautions. To his spiritual director, he rendered his monthly "account of conscience," acknowledging his faults and difficulties with the candour of a small child. Although the sequestered life he was compelled to lead at Khor-Melang was a kind of non-stop Retreat, he always insisted on "going into Retreat" once a year, according to the rule, when one or other of the Fathers would come over and put him through the exercises. Prayer was the secret of his fortitude, that interior prayer which can transform the rough substance of our nature and steady the weakest nerves.

To be resigned! It is not difficult to say yes while some temporary storm is passing over our heads. But to say yes and go on doing it for years: where does one find strength for that, save in a sustained spiritual awareness, in that abiding sense of God's presence which wraps us round, and keeps the heart warm whatever befalls? A life of dedication and devotion, the dedication and devotion of the mariner's compass which, amid all the agitations of wind and waves shaking the vessel, keeps on an even keel, remains steadfast and unswerving, in its loyalty and allegiance. Schooled as he had been in this practice from his earliest years, he had no great difficulty in coming to terms with the Last Enemy. One of those smiles of his was almost enough to disarm it and turn it into a friend.

God knows, he had seen death often enough, and at the closest quarters, too, for always the dying among his lepers had the first claim on his attention. Undaunted by the sight of the havoc the last stages of the disease plays with its victims, he would kneel close to their bodies and do his utmost to ease the passing of their souls. Under the influence of his simple instructions and exhortations, many of them were only too willing to ask for baptism before the end.

Bed-time belonged to himself and he made the most of it. Reticent and reflective by nature, such sleeplessness as he suffered from he turned to account for purposes of meditation, assisted by the silence of the African nights, unbroken save for the occasional howling of a hyena and the answering barks of the village dogs. Not always, though. Among the Shilluk, when

120

the moon is at the full, illuminating the villages like some powerful arc-lamp, a great bonfire is lighted in the compound, the tom-toms begin to beat, and everybody with a movable pair of limbs gathers around for the dance.

The dancing urge and instinct is in the blood of the people, and taking his place among the performers is, for a native boy, what the assumption of the *toga virilis* was for the ancient Romans, the difference being that the Shilluk youth has to prove his right to be regarded as a man, by keeping up the dance for hours. And what a dance! Nothing intricate or involved, but only a couple of steps to right or left with a shake of the body thrown in to make up the weight. The drums are even more restricted, being confined to one interminable sound, and the musicians entrusted with the horns send their three notes booming away to the horizon. The noise, backed by the yells of the performers, continues until midnight. Anyone within miles might as well try to sleep on the roof of a jet aircraft.

Even at this time, his pen was as busy as ever.

"Years ago when I was working with my father in the Stelvio, he gave me a good tip for avoiding the avalanches. 'Look out,' he would say, 'as often as the wind blows from the south and, if you are in a dangerous place, move away from it.' All that is a thing of the past, but I still have to cope with avalanches in the shape of the quantities of letters and post-cards you keep sending me. For I can only stare at them and then say to myself: 'Come on you lazy fellow: take your pick and shovel and get them into order.'

"It is good to learn that Milan has a Cardinal, an

honour, surely, for all Lombardy. He can be relied on to behave in church, which is something, alas, that one can't say of everybody in Italy. What a bad impression some of us give! There was a Protestant officer here a while ago, and he frankly confessed that, when he and his mother were touring our country, they were scandalised by what they saw. Do you, who have the honour to be a teacher, instruct our children in this matter. Make them understand that the bad manners they would never dream of parading before their own friends and relations, are quite out of place in the house of God.

"I see from the *Osservatore Romano* that there is great talk going on about the unemployed. Never a word about the poor Africans, though ; perhaps because they are just able to make ends meet. They don't have to build battleships and munitions of war : a bow and arrow are all they need. Let me add, however, that at the moment the only unemployed person here is myself.

"Each morning, when the Mass is over, we gather together like the gentlemen we are, sip our coffee and talk Italian like anything, in case we forget our mother tongue. Then, enters Brother Gatti, a Brescian born and bred, who was a brancardier in the war and, therefore, was never shot. He is our infirmarian and an old hand at the job. He thinks nothing of going round with his syringe, three or four times a week, and giving us Christians a good jab with it."

With all his preoccupations, he never forgot those of his family who were still left to him. News of their difficulties and misfortunes acted on his pen like a spring ; and he would exert himself to bring some light into the darkness, to get them to see the trial, whatever it might be, in a supernatural context. It was their troubles he was interested in, not his own. The point-blank questions addressed to him he turned aside and carried off with some jocular remark. Of self-pity there is never a trace.

"Since you want to know how I am going along, let me say that, for more than a year now, I have been feeling something in my hands and feet that I can make neither head nor tail of. The doctor at Cairo says that the trouble is in my bones. But I haven't broken any bones ; so what ? And, it seems, that I am to have injections of a medicine with a number on it, 135, I think.

"No, no ! I am not dead yet, or anything like it. And since I will never come back to Piatta again, I can only repeat what I said when I parted from you all : *Arrivederci*, which will, of course, be upstairs. Until then, let us have a bit of patience."

11
SINGLE TICKET TO HEAVEN

IN October, 1928, four years before the end, hope of his ultimate recovery had flared up for a moment only to die down again. The doctor in attendance began to put him through a course of injections, using an ingredient known as Oil of Hidnocarpur. This had already been known to perform wonders, and it was fully anticipated that Joshua would be able to use, or at least to move, his fingers in three months. It had antiseptic properties which acted powerfully on the infected bloodstream. But it was not to be. Eventually there was a rapid deterioration. His face became disfigured : feet and hands developed running sores.

While this was a source of disappointment and distress to everybody else, the patient went on being his usual self, covering things up with his usual jocularity. Years before, he had written home to tell them that he was "studying to make a hole in the wall of paradise" and when he said goodbye to them before setting out for Africa, his last words were : "See you again up above." Now, when his sufferings began to be intensified, he insisted he was only earning the money with which to buy a ticket to heaven.

Running sores or not, there was no interrupting his correspondence, nor yet the keen interest he took in the concerns of those he was writing to.

"You know those big nails you find in the beams of an old house : you try to pull them out and they won't budge. As far as health goes, I am like those nails. I really must be made of cast-iron. The only difference is that, unlike the nails, I am on the move all day. I get up at dawn, make my meditation, and then hear Mass along with the servant who looks after me, and a few of our converts. Afterwards, we go out on to the veranda, sip our coffee and have a good chat.

"You will be interested to hear something about my kitchen-garden : potatoes, beans, tomatoes, lettuce —all doing fine. I have just put in a row of lemon seedlings, as well as some plants called guàfa (guava) which produce a fruit like our pears. The natives have been laughing at me and saying I shall never live to taste them. Still, one never knows. Perhaps if the guavas hurry up, I might manage it.

"It is a wonderful thing to be alive ! Today I renewed my oath of obedience to the Verona Fathers, and you just can't imagine how happy a person can feel at renouncing his own will and independence, and all the things the world outside has to offer. To tell the truth, I myself had no idea of it until the actual experience came along."

Common prudence might have been expected to keep everybody away from the Black Hell of Khor-Melang, apart from those whose duty it was to be or to go there. But common prudence plays no very prominent part in the average person's life : it might get in the way. And almost any other motive will send it flying to the winds ; the satisfactions of the moment, greed, ambition, even the urge to show off. At all events, the time came when the leper-colony became a small-scale place of pilgrimage, with Joshua as the centre of attraction.

"We used to go to see him," one of the Nuns writes, "impelled by a feeling of veneration, as though we were visiting a living saint. What he had to say sank into our souls and sent us on our way, strengthened in spirit and more ready to accept our trials in the interest of the good cause."

For anyone passing through the district, whether priests, brother, sister or officials, a visit to Joshua Dei Cas came to be the recognised thing, not unlike the visit to the tomb of the Apostles pilgrims to Rome make as a matter of duty. The confrères with whom he laboured at Tonga, Lul and Detwok, brought him reports of the progress of the missions. They even turned to him for advice in their material difficulties. In 1932, the Nile rose higher than usual and ruined the drainage system in the marshes in front of Detwok. The brother-in-charge, knowing that Joshua was an old hand at dealing with floods and marshes, wrote off at once in a kind of panic. The navvy who had helped to keep the Stelvio Pass in order calmed him down with a few matter of fact instructions.

"The flooding you speak of is no new thing, as I have good cause to remember. Any of the older men of the Shilluk tribe will tell you that it happens every seventeen years, and is always followed by an even higher flooding the year after. The reason is that the White Nile, at stated times, can't get rid of its surplus water at one flooding; and, when the rain comes, the level goes up higher than ever. Get to work on your dam and make it as high as you can, and do it at once before the second inundation sets in."

The Superior at Detwok, seeing the extraordinary preparations being made, thought the workmen were giving themselves unnecessary trouble. When he wanted to know who had put such an idea into their heads, he was told that they were acting under the orders of Brother Joshua, absent on leave.

As some relief to the monotony of his life, permission was obtained from the civil authority to take him over to the mission-station at Wau for the greater festivals of the Church, so that he might relax and enjoy himself with the community.

"What do you think ! A Brother of ours comes along now on his motor-cycle, complete with side-car, and Yours Truly goes back in the side-car like a Big Chief. In case you don't know it, I am becoming a Very Important Person. You might say, in fact, that I am a regular Monsignore and, I may add, there never has been one quite like me. Now, as I have still some writing paper left, I must tell you that we kept the feast of St. Cecilia here in grand style on November 22nd. One of our priests came over from Wau, along with five brothers and the native band in full strength, drums and trombones and everything. Afterwards we had our lunch in the open, with home-made beer served out of petrol tins to wet the whistles of the bandsmen."

Father Anthony Todesco, who was Superior General of the Congregation from 1947 to 1959, recorded his impression in a long letter.

"I knew Joshua well, for we were fellow-novices at Savona. When I was posted to Central Africa, I got leave to visit him in the leper-colony. He came out to meet me with that big smile of his already so familiar. He had nothing on his feet except a pair of old shoes, and all the time he kept his hands under his arm-pits. His face, formerly so red, had turned purple and he had lost a lot of weight. The marks of the disease were most obvious on his neck and face. He was as composed and cheerful as ever. When I inquired about saying Mass, he replied : 'So, you wish to pontificate in my cathedral : excellent : you have my permission.' After we had talked over old times and had many a laugh at the remembrance of them, he took me out to see his hens and pigeons. Then we went on to interview the lepers, who all brightened up at the sight of Brother Joshua.

"When I parted with him, I was so overcome that I could only say : 'Brother, I leave you with your lepers and with our Lord.' His answer was : 'I am the happiest man on earth.' Those words have been ringing in my ears ever since and even now, after twelve years. they have lost none of their efficacy as far as I am concerned."

"The happiest man on earth." This most loathsome of all our loathsome diseases which, one would have thought, must inevitably contaminate the soul had, apparently, been passed over a filter-bed and purified in the process. He was actually getting comfort out of it, just as bees extract honey from poisonous plants.

It was his sister Teresina who received the last letter he ever wrote. Posted a week before his death, it might have been penned by a man in the best of health and spirits, with years of life to look forward to.

"When I saw that little scrap of one sheet you sent me, I got into a paddy. Don't you know that the ships that carry your letters across the Mediterranean are capable of carrying thousands of tons of cargo ? As for me, I'm in bed with a fine dose of malaria. If I were to die of it, my leprosy will feel that it has missed the bus. Greetings to all of you ; uncles, cousins and so forth. Let everything be as God wants."

Writing to Italy at this stage, one of the Fathers enclosed a photo of the stricken man, in case his life might one day be written, remarking : "It is pitiful : he looks like Job." Joshua, writing to Italy about the same time, was concerned about nothing except the misfortune that had overtaken one of the missionaries. This was Brother Corneo, who suddenly collapsed with malaria before he had been in Africa a year. It was a serious case, complicated by Black Fever and complete prostration. In the early days, three-quarters of Bishop Comboni's companions were victims of this malady, and although a lot had been learned since then, it was still a thing to be reckoned with as a killer-disease. Brother Corneo's temperature reached forty-one degrees centigrade, and the doctor declared that nothing but a miracle could save him.

Joshua rose to the occasion. In the chapel at Khor-Melang, before the Blessed Sacrament, he renounced all claim to his life on condition that Brother Corneo was saved. He was taken at his word. That very night the malaria shifted its ground. Brother Corneo began to mend and Brother Joshua went down with the same complaint which, within twenty-four hours, sent his temperature up to forty degrees. The germ he had contracted in the marshes at Tonga, lying dormant for all those years, had reasserted itself. He was so ill that the doctor ordered his removal to Wau. It was a sad moment for his poor lepers, most of whom gathered round to bid him goodbye.

In the midst of his religious brethren, he rallied a little ; but, on being told that prayers were being said for his recovery, he bade them rather pray that he might die a holy death. To the Superior who assisted him, he divulged his secret :

"I offered my life to God in place of Brother Corneo's. He is young, full of energy and of some use to the Order. I have always been a bungler, and now I am no better than a broken-down wheel-barrow, past repairing. I can be nothing but a burden to the community. Therefore, it is better as it is. This evening I shall be in heaven."

Towards eight o'clock on the same day, he who had been surmounting obstacles ever since he left school, the enclosure wall at Verona included, came to grips with the final one. During the anointing, he answered the prayers firmly and serenely, holding fast to the crucifix he had received on the day of his Profession. The Papal Blessing was given, and at ten o'clock on December 4th, 1932, the festival day of St. Peter Chrysologus, he entered into his well-earned rest. It was not death *à la mode*, but death looked full in the face and treated with respect, greeted as it was greeted by St. Francis of Assisi, whom, in many ways, he closely resembled : Welcome, Sister Death !

He was fifty-two. At the same hour and under the same roof, Brother Corneo made a complete recovery.

The funeral, which took place the next day, was more like a triumphal procession than anything else. Christians and pagans from all parts made for the church, and passed one by one round the *chapelle ardente* to take their last look at him. It was an endless chorus of praise and admiration summed up by a constantly recurring : "How good he was. Oh, how good !"

And the lepers.

"During the days that succeeded, I visited the colony

131

regularly. Poor people ! They looked lost, like sheep without their shepherd. They were never done saying how good he was. 'He always had something for us when he went round, food, fishing-hooks, pack-thread, salt, tobacco ; and such kind words as well. Who will take care of us now ? Who will keep as company ? Oh, he was a saint all right !' "

The news of his death spread quickly through the mission-stations and reached Italy in due course. The newspaper *Le Vie del Bene,* of Morbegno, published a leading article under the heading The Hero.

"There is no need to think of Joshua Dei Cas as a kind of superman, a Knight Errant terrible in his daring, with a stubborn and unconquerable will. These are childish imaginations which are apt to cling to us when we are grown up, and blind us to the fact that heroism, as the world understands it, is often a mere matter of chance or luck. But these were not the factors that led this Brother to devote his last painful years to the lepers in far away Central Africa. No ; this man was none of your legendary heroes. He went into the fray armed with nothing except his own holiness."

And his missionary brethren.

"As often as I try to pray for the repose of his soul, I almost find myself reciting the *Gloria Patri* instead."

"When I was studying Theology in the seminary, I often went to my confessor for some advice as to my spiritual difficulties. He invariably pointed to the life of Brother Joshua, as much as to say : You will find all the answers here."

"As regards myself," said Father Michelon, the Superior at Cairo, "from the time of his death, I have never let a day go by without entrusting myself to his intercession."

"Several times," writes a lay-brother, "I have visited the room at Khor-Melang in which Joshua spent those sad and lonely years. I never came away without feeling the better for it. Everyone here is convinced that he deliberately sacrificed his life in order to save the life of Brother Corneo, and all cherish the hope that one day he may be raised to the altars of the Church."

"It would not surprise me," was the testimony of the Vicar Apostolic of Khartum himself ; and he added, "You will see : before long, they will write his life."

With this in view, a beginning was made at gathering together all the relevant documents, and his two surviving brothers forwarded sixty-five of the letters he wrote from Africa and elsewhere. As for his canonization, if that ever comes to pass, he will take his place among the great lay-brothers of all time ; alongside Alphonso Rodriguez, Gerard Majella, Martin Porres, and many more whose names are recorded only in the Book of Life.

*   *   *

"Santo Cielo ! What's the meaning of this ?"

And the man lying on the doorstep of the monastery did not and could not know the meaning, not the full meaning, not at the time. And judging by his whole manner of life thereafter he did not care. "Only give me your peace and your love, and you can do what you like with me." That was the bargain struck twenty-six years before. He had never haggled over it or wished that it had never been made.

By the members of his own religious family, priests, sisters and brothers, his memory will ever be cherished as one of the most precious trophies of the Institute.

To every missionary, his heroic story must serve as a consolation and an encouragement.

To the sad and suffering of mankind, the lepers above all, and to the readers of these pages, with their own quota of trials and tribulations, his message is clear and straightforward: *Per Crucem ad Lucem.* Carry the cross and the cross will carry you.

And, finally, to the *populo minuto,* the little people, to the least ambitious amongst us, he is a striking example of what can be done with a small amount of capital laid out to the best advantage. Joshua Dei Cas was a labourer, every inch of him, with no book-learning to speak of, with nothing spectacular to show in the way of self-inflicted penances, or lofty flights into the realm of the supernatural. Aspiring only to be the faithful servant of his God and his fellow-men, he followed the beaten track of small observances and reached holiness, the true destiny of every Christian.

"Then there came one who had received two talents, who said : Lord, you delivered two talents to me, behold I have gained other two. And his Lord said to him : Well done, good and faithful servant, inasmuch as you have been faithful in a few things, I will place you in charge of many. Enter into the joy of your Lord."

CONTENTS